John Preston Smith

THE BOG

The Legend of Man's Best Friend

John Preston Smith

WHAT OTHERS ARE SAYING

"This little book and its message of the love between dogs and their owners will stay with me forever."

Writers Digest judge commentary of *The Bog*, 20th Annual *Writer's Digest* Annual Self-Published Book Awards

"This story opens with a fascinating story that grabs your attention from the very first page."

Allison S., Petluxe, Cincinnati

"I didn't know at the outset just how much I would love this book, but I found it to be deeply thought provoking. I can't get the words of the wolf out of my mind."

TKS, Belleville, Illinois

"Every element of a great story is in here."

Charlie Pangburn, Evansville, Indiana

John Preston Smith

Copyright 2014 by John Preston Smith

This novel, The Bog, The Legend of Man's Best Friend, is a revised and expanded edition of the original version which was entitled The Bog, published in 2011.

All rights reserved. No portion of this book may be reproduced, stored in a retrieval system or transmitted in any form or by any means—electronic, mechanical, photocopy, recording, scanning, or other—except for brief quotations in critical reviews or articles, without the prior written permission of the author.

This is a work of fiction and names, characters, places and incidents are either products of the author's imagination or used fictitiously. All characters in this story are fictional, and any similarity to people living or dead is purely coincidental.

ISBN: 13:978-1502830326

ISBN: 10:1502830329

The Bog: Copyright 2011 by J Preston smith

ISBN: 13:978-1466446496

ISBN: 10:1466446498

Copies may be purchased and the author may be contacted at www.jprestonsmith.com.

John Preston Smith

This book is dedicated to all the special dogs that have been a part of your life and for all those special dogs yet to come.

John Preston Smith

PREFACE

I began my sojourn with dogs when I was six. I have owned, tamed, trained, handled, found, saved, rescued, bred, and buried many thousands since that time. I culminated that journey, or at least that's what I thought, with the writing of the book *14000 Dogs Later, My Life with Dogs and What I've learned.*

I had often toyed with writing another book about dogs and had gone so far as to list the topics I would discuss; many of which regard canine behavior. However, sequels are seldom successful and each time I started writing, I continued to get this feeling that I was duplicating ideas that had already made their way to the marketplace.

Further, writers of today have covered every subject about dogs from birth to death and from earth to the hereafter. All parts of a dog's body, spirit, and mind have been explored, diagrammed, and explained.

We have bred and substituted them for every human need and pleasure while loving them above life itself...all of which has been well documented.

In reality, then, there was nothing else for me to pen about dogs...that was, however, before I met Napoleon.

John Preston Smith

INTRODUCTION

The relationship of dog and man is magical and mysterious, sometimes bordering on the mystical. It can be described as uncanny. The dog has been man's protector and companion since before recorded time.

Historians say the dog was placed here to help man cope with the difficulties of life. Dogs have been child and mate substitutes and have fought at the side of their masters in battle. They hunt, seek out drugs, find the missing, and provide sight for the blind.

They have an instinct like no other animal; they desire nothing more than to please their master. By their sense of smell, or their speed and agility, or their keen sense of hearing, they have saved, soothed, and rescued man from the slightest misfortune to his deepest fear since the day they left the call of the wild.

Above all of this, though, is a sense that remains indescribable. It cannot be defined. It is the sixth sense of dogs. It is best characterized as a sense of awareness.

John Preston Smith

THE WAIL OF PAIN

The ball I am about to throw may be difficult for you to retrieve.

—Unknown

We may be but a speck in time, but at least it is *our* speck in time!

—Mother Wolf

The greatness of a nation and its moral progress can be judged by the way its animals are treated.

—Mahatma Ghandi (1869-1948)

Day 1

    There is no place like the woods that surround my home. They are dense, hilly, and full of rotting undergrowth. They are creepy in the morning fog, humid in the afternoon heat, and eerie in nighttime shadows that slowly sway as treetops move ever so slightly in the breeze.

I often walk these 70 acres seeking respite from all things troublesome. I worry about my children and grandchildren...will their life be as blessed as mine? I worry about my country...will it sustain the world's tyranny, hostility, and terrorism? And I worry about my soul...will it be as blest in eternity as my body has been on this earth? All weighty concerns.

I do not permit hunting on my property. Though posted, hunters have no compunction about seeking deer, rabbits, and squirrels that are plentiful. They climb posted fencing, set up tree stands, and use high-powered weapons against animals whose only defense is evasion and stealth.

In the midst of my land there is a thick, swampy grove where no one goes. It is a haven for snakes, root-rot, mosquitoes, burrowing critters, and fox. On my walks I see it as wide berth. In my mind, I figure it to be where wild things go to peacefully leave this world.

I call it the bog.

Adults shy from entering this area because of its obvious dangers. I think the real reason is that they fear the wretchedness of the unknown. Children would know the bog to be a place where monstrous shadows beckon the unsuspecting, and then sweep them into the inescapable whirl of slaughter.

By now, you are wondering what any of this has to do with dogs. Okay, here goes. I only ask that you give my story a chance, let's say fifty pages, before proclaiming me loony tunes. Believe me, it took lots of internal counseling before I realized I wasn't going bananas.

On one particular day, late in the afternoon, I had climbed the hill behind my house, and while aimlessly wandering the woods pondering the hereafter for my perished pet, I found a friend in a life-and-death situation...and my life changed.

I know the different barks, whines, and growls of dogs. I can distinguish their sound of pain from that of fear, joy from aggression, and acceptance from warning.

The sound I heard was none of these.

It was a mixture, running the gauntlet of every sound I had ever heard or imagined.

It came deep from within the swampy grove that I refer to as the bog. The childlike wail called to me and my compassion and love for animals lured me as if I were sleepwalking. I pushed at vines that grabbed back, waded in muck that sucked at my shoes, and fought against mosquitoes and flies the size of alligator eyes.

My grunts and groans and wild thrashings drowned out the sounds that had drawn me into this bath of bugs, briars and brambles. Five minutes later, I halted, putting everything reaching for me on pause. Perspiration burned my eyes and blood trickled from prickle scratches on my hands and arms. My clothes felt like those taken too early from the dryer...warm and damp. My feet shrunk in my shoes, wet and wrinkled. I stirred as a creepy thing walked my collar-line. I listened. Five seconds. Ten seconds...thirty. Nothing.

Like a dummy, not knowing what else to do, I called out. In fact it was more of a whisper. "Hello...anyone there?"

Anyone? *What's the matter with me*, I thought. I didn't come in here for anyone. I came in here for a wounded animal. But how do you call for a wounded animal? I knew the answer, but I had reverted to my human ways. So I did what I had done in the first place. I continued to listen.

The whine commenced almost immediately.

Through the thick growth of climbing vines and vegetation I could see a small outcropping of rocks.

Looking down I noticed splotches of blood leading in the same direction as the continued moans and toward the outcropping of rocks.

There are many colors of red, from sky-red to ruby-red. But blood-red is more than a color—it is a warning, a danger signal, and an admonition. Looking back on that day, I probably should have stopped, backed out of the bog, and returned home, like a whipped puppy, my tail between my legs. But, compassion and curiosity overwhelmed me and I began talking in a soothing manner as I continued by fight against the forest.

"It's okay, girl. Helps' on the way. Hang in there. I'm coming."

I didn't even know what I was talking too. It could be a feral dog that would attack me on sight, thinking I was the one who had shot her. Still, I plodded on.

I broke into a small opening on the inner edge of the bog. It was, in a word, breathtaking. *What a neat place to die*, I thought. The midpoint was maybe 30 yards from where I stood. A small spring-fed pond must have been a watering point for wild animals seeking safety. Two small spotted deer looked up and then sauntered into the bush on the opposite side of the bog. Thick moss carpeted the ground while sunlight filtered through tall pines.

Momentarily forgetting my mission I sat on a stump overlooking the pond and the lush meadow. I marveled at nature's hidden treasure. Unknown bugs and insects provided music as they went about their life's mission...totally unconcerned with mine.

And then she called to me again. Her whimper had changed. Now, it was softer, quieter, more guarded. I walked, almost tiptoeing, towards the source of the cry. A trail of blood droplets mixed with the rainbow colored weeds, wild flowers, and flora led to the rock outcropping.

The low-slung ledge resembled a turtle ready to take flight, literally; and under her bottom shell, curled and shaking, lay a furry ball of a pup. De'ja' vu of childhood experiences pounded at my brain. Her warning yip was more inviting than threatening and I slowly lay on my stomach, attempting to put her fears at rest.

"Hey, girl," I said, slowly extending my fist for her to smell. She yipped repeatedly, but I remained steadfast, and after thirty seconds or so, she calmed, allowing me to touch her head and ears. I scooted closer, bumping my head on the tortoise-tummy-shell, and continued talking to her. She nestled his head against my outstretched hand and, for the first time, looked into my eyes. "Hey, there," I said and she licked my hand.

I did not know how badly she was injured, nor could I see where she was hurt, but I was encouraged to see that the blood on her fur had dried.

Time is seldom friendly. Having begun my walk in the late hours of the afternoon, it was now approaching sundown and the umbrella of trees that protected the bog from direct sunlight now turned nocturnal. Darkness descended like the flick of a switch. Further, like a bolt from the blue in a dime store suspense novel, distant thunder warned of a coming storm.

I had to make a decision—and fast—if I was to get her back to the house before Mother Nature again echoed her powerful force. Either I'd have to pull the pup, or pleadingly entice her, from the crevice between the rock and the earth. I backed out from under the small boulder to consider my options.

Defensive mechanisms are part of the human psyche, and I was in full defense mode. One of the many dangers of the bog, and the primary reason it stays moist and damp, is that it sets in a valley and at the juncture of three hills, all of which shed rain waters in one, and only one direction. Yep, you guessed it.

DELUGE

DAY 1

The deluge hit with both surprise and authority. Running streams appeared instantly and I was pretty sure where I was standing, and where the pup had taken refuge, would soon be underwater. Looking around, I noticed the faint outline of a cave above the tortoise shell, and although the footing would be difficult, it would be manageable if I started immediately. Getting the pup to agree would be the challenge. I bent down to tell of her our predicament...and there she stood, on three feet, yipping, as if to say, "Let's get to it!"

"This might hurt, girl," I said as I lifted her across the back of my neck. I grabbed a sturdy vine, fought unsure footing, and scrambled upwards to the cave, praying that Mother Nature's plan did not include the two of us.

I have never left home for walks in the woods without three items: a knife, a flashlight, and matches. I read many years ago in a survival magazine that those are the three items that save lives. I carry these in a backpack, with water and energy bars. As soon as I crawled into the cave, carefully holding my new best friend, I shone the light. As best I could tell, it had been hollowed out when an immense tree had fallen. It would fit our needs perfectly, except there was a strange odor that I cold not identify. I set the pup in a dry area, gathered twigs and sticks, and started a fire...thereafter adding larger branches.

Before surveying the pup's wound, I offered her half of my snack and poured water into my cupped hands. Her hunger and thirst was evident, as was mine. She had been holding her left hind leg from the ground, and as she lay across my lap, I began to probe. She flinched but did not growl. I washed the crusted area with water and studied the wound. She had been shot in the thick portion of her thigh muscle and the bullet was actually sticking out the inside of her leg. I was not sure what to do next. Getting the bullet out would not be easy and I did not have antibiotics...and I was not sure I could carry her all the way back to the house without further damaging her leg.

"What am I supposed to do, girl?" I asked.

She did not look as if she understood, preferring instead to rest.

I stroked her back and stomach, and for the first time, through the bursts of lightening, studied the dog I was attempting to save. I would guess her to be four months of age, forty pounds, and a German Shepherd-type dog mixed with wolf...which, by the way, is like saying, "what color is white?" No dog favors a wolf more than a German Shepherd and since dogs are descendants of wolves...well, do you see what I am saying? Her coloring, hair, snout and tail reminded me of that famous German canine.

I feared disturbing her obvious trust in me, yet a greater fear urged me to take action because I did not know how old the wound was and if infection had set in. With that, and no further thought, I ran my hand the length of her body, pinched the nose of the bullet between my fingers, and jerked as quickly and as powerfully as my muscles would permit. The bullet popped free, as did a rush of blood and pus under the beam of my flashlight. That's also when I learned that the pup was a male. He barely moved under my field medical procedure, which had to be painful. I withdrew my handkerchief and applied pressure until a slow stream seeped, hopefully cleansing the wound of infection.

Dogs are not human; they are not even *like* humans, yet he deeply exhaled as if he had been holding his breath waiting for me to dislodge the bullet. He then groaned heavily, sighed, wiggled, yawned, closed his eyes, and snuggled as close to me as he could...and he slept.

I reached into my pocket for my cell phone, but it was too late. It had been ruined by the rainstorm. Fortunately, there was no one that would be worried about me. My wife, Susan, and my daughter, Susie-q, had gone on a long weekend vacation. I had opted to stay behind and take care of our aging horse, Sprocket and my Labrador, Writer. Further, I had been working on a novel that was nearing completion, and I wanted to make the best of a few days of quiet.

The storm intensified, as did the thunder and lightning, while the pup lightly snored. I watched and listened to nature's fireworks while wondering how spending a rainy night in a cave with a wounded animal could be part of God's plan for me.

I do that, you know. I can't help it. It's my questioning nature. Maybe it's my old-school Catholic background. I don't have a problem with God existing *today.* But, *always was* and *always will be* are concepts beyond my grasp. And yet my stubbornness for understanding persists because I *want*, I *need*, graspable concepts!

Back to God's plan for me. At the point I began to think about it, the Plan, that is, I realized that I was a little scared. The storm was not letting up, the thunder and lightning was not moving on, and the rush of colliding waters already covered the tortoise shell and was maybe three feet below the cave's entrance. I repeated my daily prayer, out loud, as if that would make it more sincere and accessible to the ear of God. I know, I know, I admit it, I am a hypocrite. It is my worst weakness; well, it is one of my worst weaknesses.

At the beginning of the storm, I had been thinking about what *could be.* Now, as water seeped onto the floor of the cave, I realized *what was.*

When the rain had started, I had been in defense mode. Now, I was approaching survival mode. I eased from under the pup and flashed my light around the cave, looking for a way to climb as high as possible; hoping the intensity of the rains could not last much longer. I know this is crazy, but under the gaze of the flashlight, the cave looked almost...lived in. About five feet above the floor of the cave was a naturally constructed wooden shelf formed from the roots of the fallen Sycamore.

Without second thought, I scooped the pup from the creeping water and lifted him to the ledge. I grabbed my backpack and hoisted my six-foot frame into the belly of the tree. The pup whined. I pulled him onto my lap and soothed him as best I could, telling him that everything would be just fine. In reality, I knew better...but I've already told you about my worst weakness.

My body reminded me that it was racked. My muscles ached, I shook from chills, and my eyelids weighted ten-pounds each. As the wolf pup slept, the rain halted. Thunder continued sounding with brief reminders from far away while the remaining lightening gave notice of the slowly receding waters.

Sleep was the furthest thought in the recesses of my mind. Yet, that's exactly what took over my exhausted body as the pup and I mirrored a small wolf pack many thousands of years ago, bedding down for the night after a long day of hunting.

John Preston Smith

IS ANYONE THERE?

DAY 2: MORNING

Early morning brought sunlight, the songs of birds, and a warm breeze that wrapped itself around our damp clothing, providing a wildlife wake-up call. The pup stretched, yawned, licked his lips, his sore leg, and then my face. *An interesting licking order*, I thought. He allowed me to check his wound. The seeping had stopped, there was no infection, and from his attitude, I could tell he was not feverish. I scratched behind his ears and told him he was a good boy. His return look was deadpan. Obviously, I had not made much of an impression.

I lifted him from our makeshift sleeping compartment to the floor of the cave, watching closely to see how he treated his wounded leg. Gingerly, he touched it to the ground, slowly balanced on all fours, and then walked cautiously in circles. The limp was evident, but there was no groan as he moved. I doubted my recovery could be as immediate had I been shot in the leg.

The chilly morning and the sounds of Mother Nature welcomed us and we slid on drying mud descending to the floor of the bog.

"Well, boy," I said, "where do we go from here?"

If he were a stray needing a home, I would welcome him. However, if he were lost, a grieving family might be going door-to-door at this very minute, searching for him. I figured it to be his choice. I hugged him warmly, stroked his thick coat, and kissed him on the forehead. Not knowing if I'd see him again, I said, "It's too bad we can't share our story with anyone." *How odd,* I thought. We humans know dogs can't respond and yet we continue to make statements as if they could. Okay, okay. Yes they respond to *sit, stay, down, heel,* and *come,* and rightfully so. They'll even react to "ya wanna go for a ride?" or "ya want a treat?" or "go get your leash and we'll go for a walk."

But, expecting a response to "It's too bad we can't share our story with anyone," is, well, ridiculous.

"So this is it," I said. "I'm just over the hill there," I pointed "Feel free to visit anytime."

With that, I backed away, stumbled over a rock, caught my balance, and headed for the opening in the bush that would take me from the bog to the hill towards home. I was anxious to bathe, eat a decent meal, and nap in the luxury of our king-size bed.

That's the precise and exact point my life changed.

"Thank you," a voice said as clear as the sound of last night's thunder.

I turned. At first startled, wondering who was joking with me. Obviously, the pup's owners had tracked him into the bog and were yelling their appreciation.

I paused, waiting for someone to reveal themselves.

"Hello there," I spoke.

Nothing.

"Is anyone there?" I wondered if I had imagined the voice. "Spooky," I said to no one in particular.

I surveyed what lay before me. The birds had quieted; a cool breeze brushed my face, while the sun's rays, filtered by trees, provided intermittent glimpses of a floating rainbow, a remnant of last nights storm. The pup was not in sight. He had found his way into the bush, or was hiding.

I waited, not wanting to attempt to leave again, until the puzzle before me was solved. In sales, he who speaks first, loses. So I continued to wait.

Movement in the trees on the opposite side of the bog broke the quiet. Unconsciously, I slid my hand into my pocket, fingering my knife. As movement in the trees increased, I started back-stepping, ready to dash for safety. I had forgotten that the wall of bush surrounding the bog did not present an easy and speedy escape.

A gray wolf walked into the clearing! She was huge! She moved gracefully...as if she were walking *above* the ground instead of *on* it. A muscled chest hung over long legs and she moved with both grace and cunning. Her ears were forward, her eyes did not waver, and I felt the same increased heartbeat as that of a trapped deer. She carried her upper back, neck, and head on an even keel, parallel to the ground. I had read that the crushing power between the jaws of an adult was close to 1500 pounds per square inch. She walked straight at me. I guessed her weight at eighty-five to ninety-five pounds. My legs froze. I couldn't move a muscle. Her coat was short, dark, and dense. The fingers around my knife would not flex. *A hell of a way to die*, I thought. I've loved dogs since the first day I could walk, and now...

She walked up to me and nuzzled the hand at my side, rubbed against my leg, turned, walked about ten feet in front of me, and sat.

I felt like a puppet whose strings had suddenly been released. Was this just wild imaginings, some harsh dream filled with fantasy and make-believe?

Her body language was passive and I slowly regained by physical sense.

Inhibitions be damned, she raised her back leg and licked at herself. The pup burst from the bush, lumbered across the clearing, and dived on her...growling and nipping as if he were something to contend with. The wolf-dog rose and walked away as the pup continued to attack her tail. I cannot say for sure, but I think they hesitated, looked at me, and then continued on their way.

I sat on the ground; my legs were weak, my mind was cluttered and confused, while life around me continued as if I did not exist. Birds sang, wind rustled the trees, and rays of sunlight hop scotched along the floor of the bog. Just an ordinary day in no-man's land.

I gathered my wits and backpack; rose from the ground, took a final survey of the scene, and for the third time headed for home. After turning my back, I hesitated, wondering, hoping, expecting—something. Nothing unusual, like a voice in the wind, ushered forth.

My trip out of the bog and into solid sunlight was much less stressful than when I had entered. Don't get me wrong, the waters did not part, but the vines and briars seemed more forgiving and I broke free of the bog's grasp with very few scratches and cuts.

Walking down the hill to my house, I whistled. Moments later, Writer, my black Labrador Retriever, came bounding as if I had been away for thirty nights instead of one. She loves going on walks with me, but when no one is home, I leave her behind in alarm mode. She almost knocked me down, her excitement fueled by hunger, having missed last evening's and this morning's meal. However, her demeanor quickly changed. The scent I carried raised her hackles—her body stiffened, and her sniffs up and down my pants were short and loud. She blew her nose, clearing out the old scents while making way for the new.

She then added to my day of surprises. She stepped past me, looked directly up the hill I had just descended, and howled. I had never before heard the sound that came from her. There was wildness in her eyes. Her body was rigid and stark still and she was leaning so far forward on her toes that I thought she would fall.

I looked in the same direction, wondering at her response to the scent of my pant leg. She howled again, more powerfully than before. I listened intently, struggling to hear a response. And then, faintly, from far away, more in my mind than in the air, a whisper of a howl returned. Apparently, having heard the same, Writer barked at me, conveying her satisfaction. I shook my head, trying to clear the cobwebs of doubt and confusion that had dominated my morning, and together we headed for home, food, and normalcy.

First, though, I feed Sprocket, our 26-year-old quarter horse. Fortunately, a small, but lush pasture had kept her satisfied while I was on hiatus. Sprocket is not long for this world and we seldom leave her in the pasture unsupervised. She took to her sweet feed like a horse possessed.

"Susie-q will not be a happy camper," I said to Writer, "if she finds out I missed Sprocket's feeding schedule. Let's just keep this between us dogs, okay?" Writer showed her interest by picking up a piece of trimmed horse hoof, and with her captured treat, she scampering out of the barn.

WHO?

DAY 2: AFTERNOON

    By noontime I sat in my computer room, staring at a blank screen. Writer lay at my feet, her tummy full, while dreaming of wild romps in green pastures with four-legged friends. I munched on the staple of real men, good ole' PB&J sandwich with chocolate milk while trying to arrange pieces of the mental puzzle that lay before me. Not only were there many pieces to arrange, but the size of each was irregular, and the most convoluted part of the mystery puzzle was the fact that I didn't even know what the assembled picture was supposed to reflect. I knew it would not reveal itself, the final picture, that is, until the most critical piece was found...and for now, it was missing...and truthfully, I feared looking for it.

    I continued staring at the screen while sensibility and fantasy dueled within my subconscious.

    Walk away, the sensible and sane said to me.

You have to find out, screamed the side of fantasy and nonsense.

I pounded my fists and rose from my chair, knocking it to the floor and shattering Writer's dreams of foolishness and fantasy. "I'm sorry, girl," I said. And boom, at that moment, in those three words, I had my answer, or rather, I had the question.

I fought the urge to walk away, to leave this alone. The urge lost. I righted my chair and sat, allowing my mind to wander without constraint. I placed my fingers on the keyboard, quietly pledging to give them freedom.

"I'm sorry, girl" had immediately led me to one question—a question that no one in the history of dog and man has ever answered. Why do we talk to an animal that never answers? Okay, okay, give me a break here. Yes, there are degrees of communication. I stopped; I was getting sidetracked by sensible.

My fingers started typing, almost on their own. They pecked out a simple question—the question that I had been doing my best to avoid. It said, "Who spoke to me in the bog?"

The obvious and sensible answer is that the owner had found his pup, and not wanting to be recognized, relayed his appreciation while camouflaged by trees. But, what was he thanking me for? He did not know I had found his dog under the tortoise shell, had moved her to higher ground for safety, had removed the bullet from her leg, and had shared my food and water with her. And, if he did not want to be recognized, why did he speak to me in the first place? Finally, if the pup belonged to him, then the wolf-looking dog must also have been his, which made no sense, considering the large dog's actions of nuzzling my hand...it was almost a sign of friendship or appreciation.

My fingers lightly touched the keyboard and pecked out, "Then who spoke to me in the bog?"

Maybe it was totally unrelated to what I had done for the pup. Maybe someone was playing a trick on me, kids hiking or men hunting. But "thank you" is not a message of pranksters.

I removed my fingers from the keyboard before they could ask me the question again...and before I could seriously consider the third possibility.

♣♣♣♣♣

My love for dogs is literally beyond imagination. They have been part and parcel of my everyday life since I was a six-year-old pup. In fact, that's when I crawled under my grandmother's basement steps to retrieve a newborn liter of Dachshunds...answering yesterday's de'ja' vu episode. I have trained and handled thousands of dogs, always with the goal of improving their relationship with their master, and their lot within the household of their owner.

I believe they are one of God's greatest gifts. I have often said that I believe dogs do more for humans than humans do for humans. Dogs are important characters in five of the books I have written; one of which is a study of their behavior and how we can best understand what they bring to our table as we deal with our individual life-journey. They protect, they listen, they seek, they find, they console, they rescue, they sound the alarm, and they stand ready to give their life for us.

I have trained all of my dogs in the basics of obedience, of good behavior, and to be good citizens. I have always talked to my dogs. We all do. As I said above, they listen. I need to reword that, they are *great* listeners. It's one of their finest attributes. It's also an incredible form of communication...but I'll get to that later.

You can rely on your dog to keep secrets. How many of your human friends can you really say that about? They provide a light at the end of the tunnel, daily celebrate your arrival as if you were the prodigal child, and welcome you in from the storm by warming your feet. Dogs have pulled me through the most difficult times of my life. They have sat with me when friends and family have passed. They have encouraged me when health and happiness have turned sour. And they have taken my emotions beyond the brink of control as I have returned them to Mother Earth.

If you are a dog lover, a person who breaks bread with a dog at your feet, who walks and runs with him in the city park, and whose home and life is safe because of his presence, then you too want the same answer as I. Who spoke to me in the bog?

♣♣♣♣♣

I often live in worlds of fantasy. I love movies. Not docudrama, history, or real life. I like to see the good guy shoot 50 bad guys while sustaining no more than a flesh wound. Swartzeneger, Stallone, and Eastwood have provided enough action movies for me to re-watch for the rest of my life. And I love cartoons. My childhood Saturday mornings started with Mickey Mouse, and my evolution of cartoon enjoyment has taken me to *Who Killed Roger Rabbit,* where humans and animated characters interact.

On television, animals of every species carry on conversations about subjects not significantly different than those at our dinner table. None of that is communication. It is entertainment.

In reality, inter-species communication between man and dog is extremely limited. Yes, I know, the purists may come out of the woodwork, but the fact remains, outside of the scientific laboratory, outside of a dogs' response to training, and outside the results of a dogs' instincts, there is little to suggest that we have taken any significant strides in that direction.

Let's be clear here. I am not talking about interaction between dogs—the establishment of a pecking order, the fight for and the offering of food, protection, alarm, flight, facial and body expressions, various forms of vocal signals, and all of the interactions of their society and social order.

Rather, I am talking about a communication-measuring yardstick. On the lowest end of that yardstick are forms of communication; you approach a dog that is eating and he growls, you take a dog to the veterinarian and he begins shaking, you caress that G-spot behind his ear and he moans in pleasure, or he drops the tennis ball at your feet and then backs up and barks. I could go on forever.

Further up that communication measuring stick might be: he sounds the alarm when there's a fire in the house, he protects his old friend from the needle of death, he lies at your feet as you cry over the loss of a loved one, or, you come home from a weeks' vacation and your dog lies at your feet whimpering...where normally he would greet you with bounds of joy...what is he attempting to communicate upon your return home after being gone for so long?

Then, at the top of that measuring stick, at the optimal message point, is what I call the 'actual point of contact.' By this I mean actual one-on-one communication. No science needed. No questions about what a gesture, or bark, or signal may or may not mean. No decision-making needed. It is a communication that is apparent, obvious, and meaningful.

But does that already exist? To an extent. Dogs directly communicate with us everyday in myriad ways. Teaching is communication, right? Therefore, dogs communicate with us every time they teach a lesson. Let me count the ways. They teach us humility, patience, and affection. They teach us the value of being consistent and persistent. Living in the moment; they teach us the value of time. They are not narcissistic, egotistical, or vain...they do not use mirrors. They don't get mad, get even, or cheat. They seldom hide their mistakes, like doing number two on the living room sofa, or number one on your pillow, or doing a number on the loaf of bread that you left on the kitchen table after breakfast. They communicate with us when they sound the alarm, when they protect us from harm, and when they nestle under our arm. There's hundreds, maybe thousands, of other ways in which they directly communicate with us.

Okay, okay...my naiveté might come from all of the times I go to movies and live in fantasy worlds...or from my wild and crazy dreams; or even from my flights of imagination when I sit at the computer, allowing my mind to wander in search for a solution to the quandary that the central character in one of my novels finds himself.

But, real, apparent, obvious, and undeniable communication with animals—I do not believe it is possible. If God wanted clear and understandable communiqués passing between man and dog, He would have made that as clear as the nose on the faces of Pugs and Bulldogs a long time ago.

So, before allowing my mind to wander into realms of the mysterious, before permitting the world of fantasy to command my thoughts, and before penning unfounded beliefs that would forever haunt me, I needed proof. And that's precisely what I planned seeking.

John Preston Smith

RETURN OR NOT?

DAY 2: NIGHTTIME

I have night tremors. Eerie dreams that shock me to consciousness, waking me up perspiring and shuddering. I scream in my sleep, pound holes in walls, yell for help, and often, fall to the floor. I envision monstrous shadows that suck me from my bed, drag me to the depths of the nether world, wrap me in a cocoon, and allow their young to feed on me until there is nothing left but the briefest of memories. Susan has threatened to move to another bedroom. For now, she still endures—while wearing earplugs, eye shades, and covers pulled tight around her neck. I feel like an invisible yet impenetrable bundling board separates us.

Sleep studies and hypnotism offer no solution. Sleeping pills put me to sleep, but exacerbate the nightmares. Tranquilizers hype my awareness and deprive me of sleep.

Rather than counting sheep, I go to bed with a plan, that being, to solve the problems of the day, like how to sell more books, how to get folks to follow my weekly podcast, or how to kill the antagonist in my new novel.

Tonight would be no different. The plan would be simple and straightforward. I even wrote it on the pad next to my bed. Should I return to the bog or allow the events of the last two days to slowly melt into the past. If I return, then what am I admitting to myself? And if I ignore the past, then what am I afraid to face?

With that, I turned off the light, asked my guardian angel to protect me from the master of the shadows, and closed my eyes. The last thing I remembered was Writer jumping up on the bed. She walked circles, sorting out her own plan for the night, dropped, curled her body, and slept...as did I.

RETURN

DAY 3

I awoke rested and refreshed. I did not, however, have the answer to my question of the night before. Writer had slithered her way up the bed and now commanded three fourths of the mattress, having no understanding of the bundling board concept. She greeted the morning with a stretch and yawn that seemed to double her size. Her morning breath could gag a Great Dane.

Together, we acknowledged the early morning critters that visit the various feeders—deer, rabbits, squirrels, and birds. We walked down to the pond and she took an early morning dip as I sat in the wooden swing, watching barn swallows feed on first-light flying things. An occasional large-mouth bass announced his presence with bug-seeking acrobatics. Above me, a spider awaited breakfast after working all night on her deadly invitation.

Twenty-five yards beyond the pond, amidst a thicket of maple and pin oak trees, we had buried

Bubbles, just last week. He was my 15-year-old lap dog. Born out of wedlock, front legs resembling a horseshoe, a cute little butt that swayed when he ran, Bubbles was my steadying force against life's deadlines, have-tos, and missed appointments. He weighed in at ten pounds and expressed himself like he was ten times that size. He growled at everyone and then licked the same people. He tolerated my night tremors, persisted through five years of bone cancer, humbled himself to my idiosyncrasies, and died in his favorite place— in my lap, while I watched a late night movie.

Fittingly, he died during one of mine, and his, favorite movies, *Rocky*. Knowing he was dead, I endured the final thirty minutes of the movie, simply to hear the *Rocky* theme, which reminded me of Bubbles' life. I shoveled him into mother earth that very night, not wanting to give him back, but knowing that she could now care for him better than I could. I had stayed there the rest of the night, telling Writer that she had a hell of a long way to go before measuring up to that ten-pound pooch that was a friend to both of us. He had always loved the pond where he and Writer swam together daily, so I buried him overlooking it. Now, I wished I had put him elsewhere because the sight of that brown patch of dead grass pained me beyond consolation.

I was brought back to the present when Writer left the pond and approached.

"Don't do it," I said.

She looked at me with that Labrador deadpan gaze and slowly worked her body into a shaking frenzy, spraying in every direction, including mine.

"Thank you," I said sarcastically, the irony of my words taking me back to my visit to the bog, as well as providing the answer to my question of the previous night.

I have always vacillated about fate, coincidence, and happenstance. Are events meant to be, or do things just happen? Do things happen for a reason, or is it just by accident.

Maybe I was jumping the gun, seeing something that wasn't really there, adjudging this 'irony' to be something other than what it was—a simple expression of sarcastic appreciation.

When we ask the One of Power a question, our expectation is to receive a reasonable, uncomplicated, and clear answer. And we like those answers to be short, like, yes, no, tomorrow, in two months, or, never gonna happen. Instead, what we mostly get needs interpretation, and I decided to interpret the answer presented to me as, yes, you should return to the bog. Game. Set. Match.

I left a message on my wife's cell phone, "Hey, honey, going into the woods, taking Writer, Sprocket is doing fine, don't worry about her, will call later. Love you both."

I stuffed my backpack with the normal essential items, and then added a first aid kit. I'm not sure why I did this, I just did. Writer watched, hoping to be included. She seemed satisfied as I slipped a few dog biscuits into my pack. She raced to the front door, sat, and waited—her final reminder that she hoped to be included in my adventure.

I wore jeans and a long sleeve moisture-wicking shirt. My hiking boots were still damp and smelly and they squished when I forced them around my wool socks. I sprayed myself with bug repellant and sunscreen. It was a muggy, sunny, hot day. The rains of yesterday had vanished and the air was clammy, as the sun sucked moisture from the earth. I slipped a leather collar over Writer's neck, and for good measure, put her leash in the backpack where four bottles of solid ice were already melting. A sheathed machete hung from my belt. "Let's go, girl," I said, and she bounded through the door like a kid on recess.

Before leaving on our journey, I filled Sprocket's water bucket, measured the exact amount of grain that she was permitted to have, and set a flake of hay in each corner of the stall. Then, as if food were the relief for guilt, I added extra grain to her bucket. She looked at me as if to say, "You're in big trouble, buddy."

Today's walk up the hill appeared more difficult than that of yesterday's, and I suspected it was because there was much worry, excitement, and anticipation this time. Yesterday, I was just going for a walk, no deep feelings, no added weight. Today, my thoughts were weighted down by the memory of the past two days, the struggle with what to do next, and the poorly formed plan of what I was going to do once I arrived at the bog. I felt like I was shouldering a fifty-pound bag of dog food.

Further, there is something about climbing a hill before an adventure. It revs your various internal systems, like priming a pump, and gets your cardiovascular, circulatory, and metabolic mechanisms on high alert. You breathe like you're climbing Mount Everest, and your metabolism warns that you are starving.

Writer bounded up the hill, spewing saliva and rousting bugs of all sorts into the air. Barn swallows swooped and fed, chirping their thanks as if that were the black dog's plan all along. She flushed a rabbit and would have given chase had I not whistled. "Not now, girl," I said. She stopped, looked back at me, then back at the retreating rabbit, and then continued up the hill seeking new challenges and adventures.

Nearing the top of the hill, about fifty feet ahead of me, she stopped and froze, her black back prickling like a porcupine. My dogs are never trained to attack, just to sound an alarm or to go on guard. I increased my pace until I stood at her side.

The voices I heard were indistinct. Two men bantered back and forth. I signaled the heel command to Writer, and she and I moved cautiously to the crest of the hill which overlooked the valley of the bog on one side, and the valley of my home on the other.

Behind a seventy-year-old sycamore, I recognized my neighbor and another man that I did not know. Two rifles leaned against a tree. My land is clearly posted, so hunting is not allowed.

Announcing myself, I yelled, "Hey Joe." Joe is my neighbor on this side of the valley. He owns about three hundred acres of woodland where he hunts deer year-round. Yes, it is against the law. And no, I haven't done anything about it. Joe wore a full-face beard as if that made up for his small stature. The rest of him was covered with typical hunting attire. He is friendly enough, but there is something about him of which Writer is leery, prompting my leeriness as well.

Each man grabbed a rifle before Joe responded, almost nervously. "Zat you, Bill?"

"Am I missing out on something?" I asked, as opposed to the pleasantries of "How are you?" or "How have you been?"

Joe re-rested his gun against the tree. "I tried to call you yesterday and the night before, but there was no answer," he said, as if that was supposed to explain the presence of firearms on my posted property. "You know Jonah, our neighbor from across the valley?"

"We've never formerly met." I moved forward and offered my hand to Jonah. His handshake was passive and he did not look me in the eye. He mumbled something impossible to understand and then stepped back, like a man needing extra space. He cradled his rifle across his chest. His hunting getup was not store-bought. He wore army boots, jeans, a jacket too heavy for warm weather, and a generic hat pulled low.

Writer's hair remained restless and uneasy, not yet ready to retain its normal wave from head to tail.

"Why the gun's, Joe?" my voice was edgy, but controlled. There was no need to continue the sentence. Both men knew I did not permit hunting.

"Well, like I said, I tried to call yesterday, but there was no answer." Joe was swaying his weight from foot to foot while his voice slightly quivered. "Couple nights ago, I was walking the topside fence line along the crest of the hill and I heard sounds that would curdle coffee. By the time I got my gun and re-climbed the hill, the storm was upon me and I had to go back. Then today, when I started into the valley, I ran into Jonah, who had heard the same sounds."

"And the two of you thought what?" I asked.

"Might be a bear," Jonah muttered.

"Where ya been the last couple of days?" Joe asked.

I ignored his question. "Tell you what," I said. "You guys go put your guns up and Writer and I will check out the valley."

"You goin' near the bog?" Joe asked.

"Why?"

"Cause," he nodded at Jonah, "we think that's where the sounds came from. And you don't have a gun. God knows what's down there! I'm telling you, Bill," Joe said, "If it's a gutshot bear you'll find yourself in a world of hurt without a weapon."

At this, Jonah turned and walked away.

"Jonah," I called.

He turned and looked back, his rifle still across his chest.

"I'd appreciate it if you would not carry a loaded weapon on my property."

He eyed me carefully, lowered his shotgun and fired it into the ground. Writer growled and would have lunged had I not restrained her. "Easy girl," I said quietly.

Jonas removed the remaining shells from the breach, pumped it, and pulled the trigger, showing me it was completely empty. He turned and continuing walking.

"Weird guy, that one," said Joe.

"See you later," I said and started down the slope into the valley.

"Want me to come along?" he offered.

"No thanks," I yelled back over my shoulder. Writer had watched intently during my discourse with my neighbors. Now she bounded ahead. I wondered if she would have the same exuberance if she knew a gutshot bear was waiting somewhere in the valley below.

I unsheathed my machete as we approached the bog's wall of protection. However, I easily found where I had exited the day before and the path did not seem as overgrown. I could have resheathed the blade, but kept it at my side. If you've ever seen the craziness of a gutshot bear, well, you'd understand my unease.

Writer's enthusiasm mellowed. She stayed about five feet in front of me, her ears propped high, and her nose bobbing from the ground to the different levels of scent that invaded her nose. She constantly looked back for me.

I encouraged her, "Good girl, good girl."

THE BOG REVISITED

DAY 3

Entering a corner of the bog immediately reminded me of my previous visit, and with it came all the sounds and visions that had captivated and captured me two days previous.

Everything looked the same, except dryer. As I quietly stood, taking in the unusual scene before me, I noticed that Writer had eased from my side. The closer she got to the cave where the pup and I had spent the night, the closer she crouched to the ground. Finally, at almost a crawl, she scaled the embankment and looked into the cavern formed from the fallen Sycamore. Her ears pricked, as did the hairs on her back. She whined softly.

"What is it, girl?" I whispered.

She entered the cave, out of my sight, and lightly barked for me.

Without thought of caution, I rushed across the bog, up the embankment, and into the cave, before realizing it may have been one of the worst mistakes of my life.

I slipped on the bloody floor, landing on my right hip—the one that had been replaced two years ago. The fall jarred my lower back, and a searing pain reminded me of hospital beds, bed pans, sleepless nights, and medications that would take down an African Bull Elephant.

It took me a moment to catch my breath. Writer licked my face, her expression showing concern. "I'm okay, girl. Thanks." She continued licking. I rolled over, rose to my knees and hands, and looked directly into the eyes of a panting bear cub.

"Holy Jehosaphat," I said to Writer. "What in the hell have we gotten ourselves into?" Had Jonah shot a bear cub? Would my machete be any match against an angry adult brown bear? Am I going to be eaten by a wild animal? "We've got to get out of here now, and fast," I said.

Slowly, I began backing away, my hands caked in blood and dirt. Now, I knew the source of the strange odor I had encountered when I had entered the cave the first time. This was the den of a bear!

Again, I whispered, this time not as calmly as before. "C'mon girl."

The bear cub moaned and Writer lay down beside her.

Frantically, and with as much persuasion as possible, I whispered forcibly. "Writer, come!"

She covered the distance between us in one mighty bound, briefly licked my face, and then leaned past my neck and grabbed my shirt between her teeth. She backed, lightly pulling me in the direction of the bear cub.

We all encounter different fears in our lives. Afraid of missing the bus. Afraid of spiders. Afraid of speaking in front of the class. Afraid of bullies, horror films, sharks, bungee jumping, demons of the night, and tons of other weird fears, that just don't happen.

The fear of being ripped to shreds and eaten by a crazed mother bear had never been on my list of fears, primarily because I never—in my wildest night tremors—imagined that as a possibility. Had I envisioned such a tragedy, I can assure you, it would be number one on my list of fears.

I tried to hold my ground, hoping that my shirt would shred and I could continue my retreat. But, as luck would have it, Writer had grabbed the strap of my backpack and was winning the tug-of-war. Ignoring the virtue of caution, I relented to being hauled across the bloody floor, my spinning mind suggesting that I bandage the cub's wound and then head for the hills, hopefully before momma bear returned and made our escape impossible.

I eased over to the cub. Writer was licking the wound, and when I moved her away, I could clearly see that the cub had been shot in the shoulder. Pieces of buckshot were mixed with blood. " Jonah," I said.

I pulled the first aid kit from my bag, uncorked the bottle of iodine, and grabbed a handful of gauze sponges. Writer lay beside the cub as I poured the liquid directly on the wound, followed by compressing the site with the gauze.

You would have thought I had shot the bear a second time. She brayed wildly, a sound that included both fear and pain and I found myself begging her to relax, telling her that I had done the best that I could, that I thought she would be fine, and that Writer and I needed to get the hell out of there before all the animals of the wild descended on the cave and ripped us to shreds.

The sound of smashing trees shattered my plan. For the second time in three days, I found myself saying what I feared would be my final prayers, while at the same time I assured Writer that I would not go down without a fight. I withdrew my machete and found myself hoping that Jonah and Joe would magically appear with guns blazing so that Writer and I could survive both the bog and the momma bear, with promises never to return for as long as I live.

Again, the cub called for her mom. I scrambled to the shelf where the wolf cub and I had slept two nights previous. I called to Writer and she bounded up the incline. Moments later, momma bear entered the cave, her massive body seeming to extend from wall to wall. Pulling Writer, I scrunched to the rear of the shelf as much as possible, each movement backward taking us deeper into darkness. Through the dying roots I could see the monstrous head of the bear as she raised her nose into the air, searching for the scent that invaded her home, and for the culprit that had hurt her cub.

Finding our scent, she roared with such rage and fury that the walls of the cave could have exploded. My heart almost burst in my chest and my body became so limp that I could not hold onto the machete. Knowing that I was going to die, my mind, soul, and body started shutting down, and I became helpless. *So much for going down without a fight*, I thought. Fear was killing me before the bear could. As my body slumped to the ground, devoid of all feeling, my eyes caught two images. In the first, the bear stood on her hind legs, her forepaws on the shelf; she glared into my eyes and roared. In the second, Writer was airborne.

DEATH

DAY 3

There must be more to death than dying. It should be the answer to some magical quiz, or the explanation of some complex mathematical equation, or the solution to a problem taken to the nth degree multiple times and then squared.

There ought to be pain beyond explanation—exploding arteries and veins, the loss of a limb, a smashed pelvic bone, a shattered spine, or a crushed head.

Maybe some of us are the lucky ones. We just fall dead, or our heart stops, or our brain goes blank, or all of the nerve endings, all 520 billion of them, cease to strike.

Or we go limp from fear—overwhelming, all-encompassing, life-shattering fear. Fear that stops you dead in your tracks, paralyzing all sensation of what is about to happen. It's a fear that robs the attacker from the satisfaction of killing something, because you can't kill something that is already dead.

That bear could chew on my body all he wanted and I wouldn't protest with the slightest whimper, because I would be dead. If the bear sought satisfaction, then he'd have to track done Jonah, 'cause I think he's the culprit, the wrongdoer, the shooter. He's the one that violated my No Hunting posters, climbed the fence, tracked, and shot the bear cub that had, in turn, called upon her mother to extol a dastardly execution—on the wrong culprit!

What's the mathematical computation, the probability, or the possibility, if you will, of two animals being shot on two different days, at the same place, and found by the same guy? Who's in charge of all this? Who's moving the chess pieces? Who's to blame? Where's the voice of basic sanity? How am I supposed to interpret this craziness?

What a turn of events. I help a pup, return to see if he is still around, patch the gunshot wound of a bear cub, and now I'm the one who pays the price for all their pain and suffering. On top of that, my mind is still reeling from the thought of hearing voices the last time I was here. And so I close my eyes, wondering why Writer would sacrifice her life for me. She's always been protective, but attacking a bear—why would she do such a thing? Surely she knew she couldn't win, couldn't chase the bear away, and couldn't save my life. Are dogs that willing to sacrifice when they think that their master's life is being threatened?

I'll never know, because that's when I passed out.

LIFE AGAIN

DAY 3

When I opened my eyes, Writer was snuggled at my side. I raised my head and saw that both bears were gone. I rose to a sitting position and my head went into a vertigo spin. I eased from the shelf to the floor of the cave, steadying myself, leery and guarded like the waking of a wild animal after being shot with a tranquilizer dart. I was ready to throw caution to the wind and bolt across the clearing, through the ring of brush that protects the bog, and back to the comforts and protection of my home.

My watch beeped, indicating the top of the hour, but which one? Before looking at my watch, I glanced across the bog. It was early evening, but an overcast sky stole away the shadows. I looked at my watch, 7:00 p.m. "Let's go, girl," I said to Writer as she bounded from the cave ahead of me. And then it hit me. "Hey, you," I said to her. She stopped and looked back at me and I'd swear her expression was sheepish.

It's incredible how life experiences become fuzzy and faded in the face of the present moment. I know—at least I think I know—that Writer had attacked a bear in order to protect my life. Had I been hallucinating? Had my imagination gone rampant? Had the fear of the moment paralyzed my psyche and allowed a scene to unfold that never really happened? Or had a full-grown brown bear and her wounded cub fled from the onslaught of a sixty-pound dog? Had a fantasy vision been drawn from storage in order to protect me from going crazy?

As best I could, I scurried back up the embankment. And there, in the middle of the cave, lay an open bottle of iodine, blood soaked sponges, and a soppy puddle of mud that was sticky to the touch, carried a pungent odor, and was dark red.

I looked down at Writer, my hands on my hips, and spoke to her with full anticipation that she would answer. After all, someone had to tell me what was going on, which is exactly what I asked her. "Would you please tell me what's going on here?"

Instead of answering, she ran across the bog and into the bush, the exact opposite of the direction we needed to go. Fear is an uncontrollable and unexpected emotion, and the budding butterflies in my stomach announced its return.

My only defense against the unknown was my machete, but I was not willing to take my eyes from where Writer had entered the bush in order to find it.

The quiet in the bog was overpowering. I shattered it by calling for my dog. She did not respond.

Light began to evaporate like a forty-watt bulb slowly losing its life.

I boldly called her name again. *"Writer! C'mere, girl."*

Moments later, there was a rustling sound coming from where she had disappeared into the bush. "C'mon, girl," I said, hoping to encourage her return. But the rustle in the bush was not caused by one dog. Either it was several dogs, or my nemesis was returning.

Butterflies in my stomach had turned into raging prehistoric flying things.

She burst into the clearing. But she had companions.

Not in my wildest dreams. Not in my wildest dreams!

John Preston Smith

WILDEST DREAMS

DAY 3: LATE AFTERNOON

Romping into the bog came Writer with her new best friend, the wolf-looking pup that I had rescued and bandaged two days previous. The wolf pup was none the worse for wear and was using his back leg as if he had never encountered problem one. He jumped and nipped at Writer while playfully growling. Writer in turn dodged, ducked, and darted, using her rear end as a shield to fend off her attacker. They ran in circles, oblivious to my presence, engaged in their recreation, and amusing themselves with interaction as only dogs can, and as only dogs understand.

And then, bounding from the trees, came the mother wolf. I knew from her size and coloring that she was the same that had visited with me before.

"You have a way with us," a voice said.

I was still groggy and a bit unsteady on my feet, but my presence of mind was back to normal. Again, just as before, I looked around the bog. But now, I realized what was different. The first time I had heard a voice, it had come to me from behind a tree or from some hiding place. But, it came from someplace. I had heard it with my ears. It was sound, with volume, and a distinctly human voice. It had originated from someone's mouth, the sound was carried by waves of air, and it was received and deciphered by my eardrums.

But today, the voice did not have sound or volume. It did not come from without, rather, it came from within. In other words, it was just there, in my mind; and though it did not originate with me, still, it had origination; it had a source.

My confusion was overwhelming, and I sat on a nearby tree stump trying to catch my breath. The big wolf approached while Writer and the pup continued to play. And then, to top things off, or so I thought, the bear cub crashed through the brush and joined in the fray. I thought my ticker was going to explode.

Was I still dreaming? Had I gone bonkers? Or had I died, killed by a raging bear, and now...I was...where? I massaged my temples; my mouth was dirt dry, and I was weak with confusion.

"I've been hearing voices" is not a good thing to tell your doctor, 'cause doctors have only one answer for anything not cured by aspirin. "Let's run some tests."

And then again, maybe my imagination was running amuck. It happens, you know? People get so immersed in the problems of the day, that emotional overload kicks in and their imagination hides the problem with new and refreshing material. One would think, however, that new and refreshing material ought to be...you know...believable. And this was not a believable situation. I raised my head and looked at the wolf, who by the way, sat directly in front of me, staring directly into my eyes, exactly as she had done before.

I just shook my head, wondering, what could possibly happen next that could be any more surreal.

Movement toward the rear of the bog drew my attention as the mammoth bear emerged, flopped down headfirst, rolled onto her back and wiggled against rocks while moaning with satisfaction.

Again, I shook my head, trying to clear the cobwebs.

I know this all sounds crazy. I suspect your immediate reaction is to burn this book and deny its existence. I wish it would be that simple for me. One thing was certain. I was not going to respond to a statement that I think came to me from a wild beast. If I did respond, I would be admitting...what, that I hear the thoughts of wild animals? How is a person supposed to fend off the wiles of such thoughts?

Sensible and rational people know better. You and I know that humans do not hear the words of wild things.

But wait, I had to remind myself—sensible and rational were not supposed to overpower fantasy, and it was fantasy that had prompted my return to the bog.

Darkness was approaching. I was hungry, tired, bewildered, and wanted to go home. I rose and headed for the opening in the wall of the bush. Lightly, I called for Writer, not sure if she would come with me or not. I did not look back; rather I plodded with little enthusiasm, away from the curse of the bog.

Writer brushed my legs as she quietly passed. Neither of us spoke from that point in time until the following morning.

John Preston Smith

SUSAN

DAY 4

I was jolted awake when something pounded on my bed. My night of tremors had included hairy and bloody monsters that stole people from their homes, broke their bones to keep them from escaping, and kept them in caves. I awoke with a start, flailing my arms and screaming at the top of my voice.

Six-year-old Susie-q, never having witnessed the consequence of one of my nightmares, immediately cried.

Writer jumped up on the bed and licked her face, and Susan rushed into the room with this huge questioning look on her face. "She just wanted to surprise you," Susan said as she sat on a corner of the bed and soothed our daughter.

I made amends as best I could. It's kind of hard, though, to transition from a nightmarish bloody cave-of-death to a bed full of family and friend.

Susan fixed breakfast. I was famished, and figuring Writer to be the same, I slipped toast and bacon under the table.

"Stop that," Susan said.

There was a knock at the door and our neighbor from down the lane dropped off her daughter, Cindy.

"Can we go to the tree house?" asked Susie-q as she and Cindy bolted out the back door without waiting for an answer. Before the door slammed, Writer joined them. She has always been particularly protective of Susie. I never took that for granted and often told her of my appreciation.

As I finished eating, Susan took a basket of clothes into the laundry room.

Susan is cool. I am ten years her elder, but she is smarter than me, which makes me wonder why she married me. I had been married to my first wife, Jennifer, for 18 years. She was killed in a car crash. Three years later, Susan appeared at my door, asking, at the behest of a client, if I would like to sell my property. She was a highly successful realtor and she did not take lightly to my brisk answer, followed by the close of my door.

What I did not realize at the time was that Writer had slipped out the door and was headed to Susan's car, where her Labrador, Stanley, waited.

A few minutes later, when I heard the commotion of playful dogs, I peaked through the curtains. Susan, I was convinced, had already cased my property, knew that I had a dog, and had brought hers along as a back-up plan.

"Nice," I said to her from the doorway.

"What?" she said, her shoulders humped and her hands airborne, like any good Italian.

I had not noticed when she first appeared at my door. Now I did. She was a knockout.

"May I have my dog back?" I asked.

"It'll cost ya?" she said, almost teasingly.

"Ice tea?"

"Please."

"C'mon in. And bring..."

"Stanley."

"Stanley?"

"Stanley."

"Why Stanley? What kind of a name is that for a dog?

"It was my Dad's name."

That was good enough for me.

Susan had first knocked on my door at 4:00 p.m. At 7:00 p.m. following spaghetti and meatballs, she said. "I gotta go. Are you sure you don't want to sell this place."

"No, thank you."

"I don't blame you. It's fantastic."

We walked to her car in silence. I opened the driver's side door and Stanley jumped across to the shotgun seat. Without hesitation she asked, "Can Stanley and I come back and visit with...Writer, sometime?"

I smiled. She reached and kissed me on the cheek, got in her car and drove away. Two months later, we were married. Two years later, Stanley died after running from cancer as hard as he could. He and Bubbles are buried side by side.

There was much more to Susan than her incredibly good looks. She was sensitive, understanding, and caring. She loved nature, animals, and the outdoors. But, most of all, she and I could have wonderful talks together...sometimes, along with a bottle of sweet wine. Those talks would last most of the night. And she had a knack. If something were on my mind or if something bothered me, she noticed. This was one of those times.

"What's going on?" she asked.

I wasn't sure where to start; in fact, I wasn't sure I wanted to tell her anything. I mean, come on, I ask you...what would the most sensible, understanding, and caring person in the whole world say if I told her about my weekend in the bog? Words like foolish, crazy, dreamer, wild, extravagant, and nuthouse come to mind.

"Is it too early in the day to have a drink of wine?" I asked.

"It's ten in the morning." She crossed her arms and looked at me with concern.

"Just kidding," I muttered. But she knew.

She crossed the room, kissed me on the cheek, and motioned towards the couch. "Why didn't you call me this weekend?"

I hate open-ended questions. The ones you can answer with a yes or a no are so much easier. I looked outside and could see and hear the girls playing. It was time to learn the length and breadth of Susan's qualities of sensible and understanding. So I told her the story...the whole thing.

WHAT NEXT?

DAY 4

"Sensible and understanding" are human terms describing certain capabilities of the brain. An example of sensible would be to take an umbrella with you when rain is forecast. And example of understanding would be to know what to do with the umbrella when water falls from the sky.

The words sensible and understanding also define the length and breadth within which our minds allow us to roam.

We all understand fantasy, flights of the imagination, and the unlimited restrictions of entertainment. Daydreams can become reality as our mind's eye blinks away doubt, and we find solace in movies depicting happy endings, solved problems, and life-changing wonder.

This is all well and good because our mind knows and understands the difference between reality and fantasy. But there is a point where our minds balk. Even though we travel beyond gravity, even though the power of atoms and hydrogen is within our grasp, even though we've proven the existence of our world to number in the billions of years, still, once our reality is challenged, we quickly establish parameters, fences, guiding principles, and roadblocks. We tend to recoil at accepting the possibility of the impossible—like world peace, living forever, reincarnation, and communication with lower life forms.

And so, as I feared, Susan balked.

"I don't understand," she said. And then she tried to explain what she did not understand, which, by the way, is much more difficult than explaining what you do understand.

"None of this makes any sense. You spent two nights in the bog helping a wounded wolf and a bear cub. You could have drowned…or been eaten by a bear…hell, you could have been shot by Jonah."

"When you first came to see me because you had a buyer for my house, I could have been an axe murderer, hell you could have been axed," I said. My lousy attempt at humor, and reason, flicked a switch in Susan's brain.

"So, when are you going back?" she asked.

I wasn't sure if Susan was being supportive or condescending. I know she wanted to help me with my quandary. "I want to go back later today."

"Don't drive yourself crazy trying to figure this thing out…maybe you're not supposed to."

"What do you mean?"

"Some riddles are just riddles…there's not necessarily an answer."

Confused, "I nodded."

"I'll fix sandwiches." With that, she walked to the kitchen.

"PB&J," I yelled.

"PB&J, it is," she answered. Then, "I'll use the bread of life; I'll spread the peanut butter with the knife of good sense, and the Jelly with the spoon of destiny."

I shook my head, wondering how desolate my life would be had Susan not been a realtor.

John Preston Smith

LATE AFTERNOON

DAY 4

Expectations are like the edge of a mountain we force ourselves to walk to...not knowing until we get there whether we'll take that extra step or not. As Writer and I walked the hill behind my house, heading for the bog, I wondered if I was approaching the precipice of that mountain.

I understand the phrase "expect the unexpected," but how are you supposed to imagine the resolution of the impossible? Would you be willing to give up your life while not expecting to die?

On my way up the hill, I went through the list of reasons that this was happening to me. One, and only one answer seemed plausible—punishment. That conclusion also seemed reasonable when considering that no sane person would believe me if I told them what I thought I was about to encounter. Then again, two sane people had already accepted that what I was experiencing might be the real thing. But, one of those people was me; and the other loved me beyond understanding. That may sound like I'm batting a thousand...but then again, this is not the game of baseball; it's not the game of life...it's not even a game.

And, I'm not sure that I deserve punishment of this magnitude. As an example, making my story public might lead to recriminations of fraud, deception, and deceit. My reputation and good name would be mud. My few friends would disappear, and worse, my daughter would be emotionally disfigured beyond repair.

Those of us spiritually touched always blame the unsuspecting events of our lives on the plans of the Greater Being. "It's His plan. It's what's supposed to happen. It's the way things are meant to be. It's fate."

I'm not of that church. I'm a believer in free will. Which also means that I believe punishment is the *result* of our lives; not *part* of our lives. I believe in God...but I do not see myself any more important than the next guy. God probably sees me as the *least* of his brethren...which is okay by me...at least He knows I'm a believer, even if I am at the bottom of the totem pole to Heaven.

So where does that leave me? If I'm not being punished, then why am I in this mess? As the saying goes, "God offers salve for our wounds, but we have to have the sense to apply it."

Writer's bark brought me back to the moment at hand...and none too soon. I had wandered off the path and was near a drop-off that would have sent me tumbling into a clump of trees that surely would have broken my back...talk about the edge of the mountain!

She and I stood at the top of the hill, looking forward into the valley of the bog, and then looking back down the hill to my home, family, and the normalcy of my former life.

I knew if I continued into the valley, my life would forever be altered. I can't remember who, but someone once said, "Life is hard enough without getting in your own way." Now, as I prepared to take the next few steps of my life, I was about to trip over more than just myself.

Or I could return home, thereby erasing the events of the past four days from the blackboard of my life. There was only one thing to do. I am a believer in meditation, relaxation, and stress management. So I sat. I removed the backpack, my utility belt, and my hat. I crossed my legs as best I could, and following the tenets of yoga, I cleared my mind of clutter and opened it to the realms of universal contact. With my eyes closed, I concentrated on nothing but the songs of the wild birds.

Five minutes later, I returned from a dreamlike séance, and opened my eyes. Writer sat immediately in front of me, panting with anticipation while her tail wagged furiously. I stood, snapped my utility belt in place, put my hat on my head, and slung the pack over one shoulder.

Then, with a clear mind, I moved forward into the valley of the bog...knowing that I was putting my dreams, desires, and goals on hold while my current life was on temporarily assignment.

John Preston Smith

RETURN

DAY 4

Writer approved of my decision, bounding down the hill with the enthusiasm of a pup, as if she were answering calls that are inaudible to humans.

But too, she heard something else and slammed on the brakes, crouched, and growled in the direction of a huge Sycamore. Jonah stepped from behind the tree; his shotgun, attached from barrel to butt with a leather tether, was slung across his back. He did not wear the worn clothes in which I had first seen him. Rather, he looked like a movie depiction of Daniel Boone.

My mood of anticipation changed to one of irritation, and I was not feeling particularly neighborly.

He, on the other hand, finding himself clearly the trespasser and recognizing my growing anger, attempted to display concern for my safety.

"At night I've been hearing the wildest sounds coming from here in the valley...and worried about the possibility of a gut-shot bear and your little girl...thought I might check it out."

It was more words and longer sentences than I thought he was capable of assembling.

He un-slung his shotgun. "Bessie here is ready to solve the problem." He stroked his gun barrel as if it had feelings.

I moved with the speed that resulted from military training, grabbed his rifle, broke the stock against the Sycamore, and handed the shattered gun back to him.

He turned white with surprise.

Knowing, however, that anger is not like the color of your eyes—that is does not have to stay with you all of the time—mine eased.

I calmly told him, "Leave my land, Jonah. I will not threaten you with consequences, just imagine the worst if I catch you here again."

He did not attempt to reply. He turned and left the valley as quickly as a thief on the run. I watched until he was out of sight, using that time for blood to return to those areas of my body from whence it had drained. Interesting, isn't it, how adrenalin can shut down or rev up our bodies...and we have little to no control over its effect on us.

I turned to Writer. "You lead...I'll follow." She barked an answer and for the third time in the past hour, we headed for our destiny.

The temperature in the bog was at least ten degrees cooler than that of the outside world. Birds, rabbits, and squirrels enjoyed the nectar of flowers, grass, and berries and scurried from one to the other with the passion of a job well earned.

Their peacefulness gravitated around us and I sat on the stump of a tree that seemed to be waiting just for me.

First to appear was a deer and her fawn. If they noticed my presence, they were not frightened. They foraged for grass as they worked their way to the pond. Writer joined them for a drink. I was surprised at the appearance of the fox, but the rabbits and squirrels were not, which was a bonus surprise for me. I removed the packet of animal biscuits, the crinkling of which drew everyone's attention. Rather than standing, not wanting to intimidate them, I threw the food as best I could from a sitting position.

Though hungry, they did not charge for the prize. It was more of a meander. They ate. I threw more. They moved closer. I watched them. They were not eating with a nervous eye watching for predators. Within five minutes, the fawn picked treats from one hand while a squirrel found his way into the food bag held by my other hand.

When the food had been eaten, the animals went back to exploring the floor of the bog and I built a small fire. The warmed can of beans tasted pretty good. I had saved plenty of treats for Writer. Darkness comes early in the bog as the umbrella of trees hides the evening sunlight. Looking at my watch, I realized I had been feeding and talking to the animals for two hours, totally oblivious to the purpose of my visit—a realization which seemed to cue the appearance of the wolf.

At the moment of her entrance, I was sitting on a blanket, and leaning against the stump. She walked directly to me and lay down beside my leg. She ate a few teats that I had saved, licked at the empty can of beans, and then dropped her head into my lap as I stroked the thick, scraggly hair on her head and neck.

Funny, I thought, I had no expectations. I merely reveled in the moment. Who else, on earth, ever, had experienced what I was experiencing at this very moment? To me, being one with nature had never been more than a pointless statement that described the impossible. Humans tend to do that. Usually though, we portray or define our attributes and shortcomings by referring to the abilities of animals—abilities impossible to attain. Fly like a bird, float like a butterfly, sting like a bee, cunning as a fox, mean as a gut-shot bear.

Maybe that's what being one with nature really means—being able to fly like a bird. Or, being able to sit in a field of wonder, as wild animals feed and drink side by side, and a ninety-pound wolf, an animal as pure today as she was thousands of years ago, lies at your side, seeking nothing more than a biscuit, a companion, and a pat on the head.

As evening dawned, an indescribable peace settled across the bog. One by one and side by side, the animals dropped to the ground and curled and cuddled together, drawing and sharing body warmth against the chilly night.

I slowly slid down the base of the tree stump, moving as best I could without disturbing the wolf. She, in turn, grumbled, and then repositioned herself against my side. Writer and the wolf pup returned from their field of play. Writer sniffed the big wolf from head to foot, licked my hand, and nestled against my other leg.

The pup lay beside her mom. One with nature, we slept.

THE CALLING

Day 5

I awoke to a howling, a primal call that would raise the hackles of the staunchest spirit.

A morning mist lay about three feet above the floor of the bog and I could barely see my friends at the far side of the pond. A cacophony of calls emanated from the group, one of which I clearly recognized as that of Writer.

It was not music; rather it was musical. It was neither organized nor synchronized. It was not rhythmic or patterned.

It's meaning, however, clearly penetrated my soul and I knew with immediacy it was the call of death.

I eased to my feet and approached the group that consisted of many, and various, animals. The chorus continued with howls and moans as primitive as prehistory, and the sounds touched my soul with the purity of rapture. The sound was primordial but captivating, unsettling yet comforting, ancient but original. For the slightest of moments, the nature of which may also have been primitive, I nearly added my voice to this feral call of nature...but the sounds stopped.

The built-up air eased from my stomach as breath, rather than a howl, and Writer ran to me as she had every other morning of her life. All the animals, save the big wolf, slowly evaporated into the walls of the bog, the quiet of their mournful voices now apparent in their sluggish motion.

Animals die so much differently than you and me. It is an acknowledged fact that many animals seek a place of hiding when death approaches, and I strongly suspected that a member of this group had, during the night, departed in search of its final place of earthly rest. A prayer of peace escaped my lips and the wolf looked at me; her brows wrinkled and her ears perked forward.

The aura of calm within the confines of the bog began taking a softer line as the mist melted into the air, and the voices of Mother Earth again greeted the day as they had since the dawn of time.

My stomach growled and I opened a cereal bar and gave half to Writer. Again, the wolf watched; so I gave her the other half. I broke open a second energy bar and before looking at either dog, I plopped it in my mouth and washed it down with a bottle of water, fearful that my good intentions would once again win over the pangs of hunger in my stomach.

I sat on the tree stump while surveying the happenings of the past few days. It took two words to describe: mind-boggling. But I did not come back to this place to be mesmerized by the past. Rather, I wanted to know if the past were fantasy or fantastic. If it were fantasy, then somehow I needed to know what conniving power had overtaken my body and mind.

If it were fantastic, I wanted to know why me, why now, and why at this place. My granddad had a saying: "It's up to each of us to get out of our cage."

Well, granddaddy, I thought, *I wonder if this is what you had in mind.*

The wolf and I sat staring eye to eye. I have always talked to my dogs. All dog lovers talk to their dogs. None of us, in the history of forever, have expected a response. Maybe, I was thinking, that's the reason we have never gotten one. *Nothing ventured-nothing gained*, I thought to myself, deciding at that moment to take a giant step of foolishness.

"Are you the one who spoke to me?" I said directly to the wolf.

She stared at me. Her ears pricked forward. Her frown was slight. Her eyes remained steady.

I waited.

There was no reply.

I tried again, now starting to feel foolish, hoping no one was hiding in the trees doing their best to stifle laughter.

"Did you thank me for caring for your pup?"

She sank to the ground and crossed her front feet. Then she yawned. I thought for sure she was going to flop over on her side, close her eyes, and sleep.

Another of granddaddy's quips came to mind. "If you don't know what to look for, how will you know when you find it?"

So I plowed forward. "Did you say, 'You have a way with us'?"

She rolled to her back and began wiggling like a worm cut in half. She moaned with pleasure as she found the spot that itched.

"We all lack certain abilities...thank God we don't lack imagination." Granddaddy again.

All of a sudden I was more embarrassed by my far-fetched imagination than my bumbling ability to speak.

A crash of thunder followed the crack of lightening in a sky that was blue and cloudless. The wolf rose back into a sitting position, scratched her ear with a hind leg, and looked at me.

"Yes, yes, and yes," are the words she spoke to me.

SHOCK

DAY 5

Expectation covers a wide range of life's experiences. At one time or another we expect to laugh, cry, fight, give in, love, play, obtain a good job, win, loose...the list could go on and on.

We also have hopes and dreams. We hope to meet the perfect mate, hit the lottery, to stay healthy, live a long life, have children, become grandparents, and die peacefully with our family at our side. It's an equally long list.

Occasionally, we experience the totally unexpected by receiving bolts from the blue, bombshells, impossible revelations, and surprises from beyond the Milky Way galaxy.

I did not fall within any of these categories when those thee words—*"yes, yes, and yes"*—scrolled across my brain.

Rather, my worst weakness jumped into the fray. Had I been one of the 12 Apostles, they would have referred to me as Thomas, the Doubter. I can't help it. I have a difficult time accepting as true those things that I do not understand. I wonder why the hand of pain and suffering is dealt to so many good people. I wonder how atoms explode, how airplanes get off the ground, what controls gravity, why stars don't collide, and why no one stopped the Holocaust, WW II, and the Vietnam Conflict.

And now this; a wolf communicating with me. If ever I should doubt, it is surely now. I should doubt what I want to believe, I should doubt that which is clear and present, and I should doubt my sanity. But I can not.

For some reason—and surely there is reason behind what I am experiencing—I have been chosen to be here at this very moment in time.

This is not happenstance, coincidence, chance, or accident.

Rather, this is planned, pre-ordained, and designed. By whom, I have no idea. But the conspiracy is as real as the existence of man's best friend. And, this is not fantasy; it is as genuine and as fantastic as truth, goodness, and love.

Our eyes locked and I moved any of my remaining doubt to one of the back cubbyholes of my mind. I verbalized another question. She clearly understood my words so I was not going to test her by imagining my queries as if we were going to communicate through mental telepathy. I could deal with her passing her thoughts directly to my mind. In fact, I was more comfortable with that than I would be by hearing and seeing the words come from her mouth like some doctored You Tube video.

"Do wolves and dogs have names?"

"I am Napo. My pup is Bonj. Again, thank you for caring for her...and for tending to the cub as well. I do not understand why someone would shoot our young."

Her words scrolled across my brain and I rushed to ask another question before the phenomenon passed. "Why me?"

"Because you are one of the few who understand."

"Understand?"

"Our plight, our plan, our destiny." A butterfly settled on her head, she looked up, and I swear I saw her shrug. She shook her head, and the butterfly took to flight.

I wanted to say that I did not believe this was happening...but it was, and it was way beyond cool. Was I enthralled? Maybe. Ecstatic? No. Panicky? Again, no. In the moment? Yes. In fact, I was almost relaxed. My rear end had had enough of the tree stump and I moved to the ground. I started to ask another question, but before it escaped my lips, I stopped. I did not want the following questions to be about her pup, and the bear and her cub, and their names and ages, and other questions of minor importance.

That's not why this meeting was planned. The issues before us had to have a greater meaning than obtaining the superfluous.

She just watched me...waiting for the next question.

"Why do you say that I am one of the few who understand?"

"You wrote The Prophecy of Canine.*"*

"I did...but, how...?"

"How did that story come to you?"

"It has always been in my mind."

"It is closer to the truth than you know."

I felt a constriction in my chest. How could she know what I had written—or about my love of animals? *Wait a minute,* I thought, *this is getting out of hand.* How could a wolf know anything about me? If she wants to discuss how the world mistreats dogs, well, okay. I accepted that premise before coming here today. In fact, she could discuss that with any number of humans who harbor a passion for pets.

But this was different. It was personal. It was me that Napo wanted to communicate with all along. I had become so enthralled with the whole idea of what was going on in the bog that I had never considered that wolves are not even indigenous to this part of the country.

The constriction continued. I tried inhaling and exhaling deeply and slowly. I felt flushed, my hands began to perspire, and little whirly things danced and tumbled against my inner eyelid. And then, she said:

"We are aware of the many thousands of dogs that you have trained and handled. And we are aware of the wonderful and touching stories that you have written about us. Your compassion and understanding about who we are and what we stand for could not have come to you other than by the hand of the One."

In my mind I knew this had to be a dream—maybe even one of my night tremors. Foolishly, I tested her. "And your favorite story that I wrote was...?"

"The Stray, she said without hesitation.

We all have our individual and personal "great fears" in this world. One of mine is water. To me, the definition of swimming is an attempt to stay alive while in the water. All of a sudden, sitting on the ground in the bog, I felt like I had just been thrown into the deep end of the pool and I was slowly sinking. What was I supposed to take from what Napo had just said to me?

Was she a mind reader, or had she been sneaking into my house late at night, stealing my novels and reading them under the light of a full moon before returning them, and then dashing off to God-knows-where before my family and I faced the morning sun? Pretty crazy thinking, right?

Or did she possess some bizarre absorption technique whereby everything that exists, also exists for all to see and know, which means that every thought, spoken or not, written or not, becomes available on some universal plane of knowledge for the edification of all living things, excluding humans, of course. Crazier thinking, right?

Still...why me?

Sure, for many years I've written about dogs and their service to mankind. Yes, I believe they are a special gift from God. They are incredible substitutes: mate, child, and empty nest syndrome. I have called them magical and mystical, mythical and mysterious. And yes, I believe dogs do more for humans than humans do for humans.

But surely, others have penned the same thoughts, and with greater verbiage than I could ever muster.

I am not a dog psychologist and I am not a canine behaviorist. I merely understand dogs for what they are—a species that was personally selected by God to watch over us, to guard and protect us, to listen to us, to guide us, to offer sympathy, companionship, loyalty, and devotion.

They are descendants of the wolf, willing to lay down their lives for us, and they are, beyond any comparison, our best friend.

I will take these beliefs with me to my grave.

But surely, these values are not worthy of pure and simple animal communication. How could that be?

"Having a tough time dealing with this, huh?"

"Don't be cynical," I said. "I don't think man is equipped to deal with this kind of revelation everyday."

"Do you believe in the Bible?" She was still starring at me.

I was totally caught off-guard with her question...but then again, maybe I shouldn't have been. Weakly, I answered, "Yes."

"And divine inspiration...do you believe in divine inspiration?"

"Divine inspiration? Did you say divine inspiration?" I was losing it. "What does that have to do with the relationship between wolves, dogs and man?"

The wolf yawned and then looked around almost nonchalantly...as if dealing with me was going to be more difficult than she thought. She rose, stretched, turned and walked towards the pond.

I wasn't sure what I was supposed to do. Maybe I had offended her. Maybe her questions were a test and I had failed and she had decided I was not the one.

Then, she stopped and looked back at me. "This way."

I jumped to my feet and caught up with her as fast as I could. I thought about apologizing, didn't, and instead followed her like a whipped puppy.

At the pond, she crouched and drank, her long tongue lapping the sweet nectar into her mouth. Largemouth bass fed on insects, as did swallows and dragonflies. Moments later, we were joined by Bonj and Writer, who dashed the serenity of the moment with their wild dives and tumbles into the water. I found the shade of a tree and removed water from my pack.

Napoleon—I had not told her that I had chosen that as her human name—rolled on the ground, trying to defend herself from the attacks of Bonj and Writer. Five minutes later, the three lay in the grass and slept while the tree-filtered rays of the afternoon sun sucked pond water from their coats of hair.

I, in turn, tried to filter through the happenings of the day and found myself lost. How could she know of my books, or the Bible, or divine inspiration? Was she telling me that animals do have souls, and that they have an afterlife, which, by the way, is a theory I have espoused for many years?

Okay, okay, I understand your doubt...but please let me explain myself. After all, you've stuck with me this far...just give me a few more pages.

RANDOM THOUGHTS

You think dogs will not be in Heaven? I tell you, they will be there long before any of us.

—Robert Louis Stevenson

If there are no dogs in Heaven, then when I die I want to go where they went.

—Will Rogers

DAY 5

Anyone who loves dogs as much as me wonders what happens to our pets when they pass away. Do they have a soul? Do they go to Heaven? Is there any Biblical passage giving us a glimmer of hope about their afterlife. And if so, what might that be?

I answer that question by asking myself what aspects of life are most meaningful to me. What do I treasure most about this wonderful earth that has been given to us by God?

If I had one day to live, how would I spend it? (I can assure you my dog would be included). If my house were on fire who or what would I attempt to retrieve?

(My family, my dog, and my family treasures, in that order). If the world were to end in the next eight hours, what memories would I want to relive? (Surely this book answers that question). If I were to die and go to Heaven, in addition to seeing the Lord God, who else would I hope to see? (My family, my friends, and my dogs).

I believe that God placed us on this earth for two reasons: 1) to live a life worthy to attain Heaven and 2) to enjoy the wonders of the world that He gifted to us.

Those wonders are too myriad to list. But I will tell you it is impossible for me to think about Heaven without envisioning the wonderful gifts that we enjoy here. Why would God provide happiness here that would not be duplicated there?

If the gates of Heaven are not open to dogs, then how about the giant sequoias, or roses, or hills and mountains, or endless oceans, or quiet valley streams? Can you imagine Heaven lacking these marvels?

How about the Seven Wonders of The World or The Grand Canyon, Stonehenge, the Great Wall of China, the Leaning Tower of Pisa, the Taj Mahal, the Roman Coliseum, the Old City of Jerusalem, the Polar Ice Caps, or the Vietnam Wall?

How about the largest ocean animal, the blue whale, or the largest land animal, the African bull elephant? How about dogs?

When I imagine Heaven, I see myself surrounded by God and all the wonders of His earth, including our canine friends.

Is this biblically sound? Probably not.

Is it biblically sound to say that Heaven is a reward for a life well-spent? Absolutely. Does a life well-spent include companionship, affection, loyalty, dedication, dependability, friendship, courage and part of the family? Yes.

No one has returned from the afterlife to let us know what it's all about. We don't know if there are hills and valleys, lush vegetation and rolling landscapes, rain forests and wildlife, and all the friends of God.

But I have to tell you, it's hard to imagine this place of beauty without my canine friends. After all, they've been a positive force for me while I've been here. Who's to say they don't deserve Heaven as much as I do?

The defensive answer for most of us through the years is dogs do not go to Heaven because they lack a soul. This is not saying they don't have soul, rather, it is saying they don't have *a* soul.

It might be interesting to consider the theory of one of the great thinkers as we ponder this subject matter.

The prized student of Socrates was Plato. The prized student of Plato was Aristotle. I mention this lineage of names for a reason. Aristotle's opinion of the soul differed substantially from his predecessors. He envisioned three levels of soul within nature.

The first level, he called the *nutritive soul,* for which he attributed to be the driving force for all plant life.

The second level, he called the *sensitive soul,* a force inborn in animals, which are aware of their environment. He believed animals had feelings due to their enhanced form of soul.

The third stage, he called the *rational soul,* unique to humans. A force providing rational thought.

Don't get me wrong here. I'm not searching for reasons to contradict any religions position regarding the family tree of God, man, soul, and Heaven.

It has always been man's hope that something wonderful begins at our death. We accept this on faith. Like I said above, no one has returned to confirm that theory to be fact. And so we tend to grasp at straws, anything that will support our hope that there's a better life yet to come.

Here's the point. There are mysteries that we *all* wonder about—even Aristotle. If it takes a soul to get to Heaven, and if dog's have souls—at least according to Aristotle—then maybe dogs *do* go to Heaven. And if they don't go to Heaven, then surely, they reside on the outskirts of its gates.

So, now you know where I stand regarding dogs, their souls, and their afterlife. I know it's a stretch, unless that is, it turns out that they have their own version of the Bible, and, after meeting Napoleon that wouldn't surprise me at all.

And finally, speaking of the Bible, what if it were updated, rewritten, or modernized, at least to the extent that it could speak more clearly to today's believers.

I am not suggesting any changes whatsoever to the Old or New Testament. But since it is appropriate to say that the church is here to serve the people—by that I mean doing everything in its power to assist us in catching the train to a Heavenly afterlife, as opposed to the people being here to serve the church—then maybe some modern day additions could be considered.

During the writings of the Old and New Testament, dogs were hardly an afterthought. During that time they were not strongly imbedded in the family life of the people; nor were they socially accepted as protectors, guardians, and companions. Over the past two thousand years, that has changed drastically. Just look around. The heroics of dogs today are literally beyond anything considered by the divinely inspired writers of the Bible.

Here's the question:

If the Bible were updated today, would writers be divinely inspired to suggest, because of what dogs do for us today, that a Heavenly kennel awaits them?

And here's the test:

How would your world, and the world of divinely inspired writers, be affected if, upon waking tomorrow morning, there were no dogs in the world?

John Preston Smith

EVENING

DAY 5

I'm not sure what my expectations were regarding time, but hunger pangs forced the opening of sandwiches, and the aroma brought the three dogs clamoring. I was amazed at Napoleon's ability of being 100 percent wolf, and moments later, sitting in front of me, staring, and philosophizing. At the moment, however, her eyes were wide, her brows raised, and her ears jutted forward in the same manner and anticipation of Bonj and Writer. Ahhhh, the great equalizer—food!

Bonj and Writer playfully fought for crumbs, while Napoleon continually nudged my arm for more of the main meal.

"I didn't know wolves liked PB&J," I said, not really expecting an answer in front of the others. She did not acknowledge my statement preferring to yipe at me as if begging for more.

When we were finished, I tidied up the area where we had eaten, zipped up my pack, and slung it over my shoulder.

While Bonj and Writer drank at the pond, Napoleon spoke her final words of the day.

"*Tomorrow is the last day we will talk.*"

"I'll be here early," I said to her as she trotted to the pond.

I whistled and Writer came without hesitation. Then, together, we headed into the bush that protected a world that no other human knew about but me.

HOME

DAY 5

When Writer and I arrived home, Susan was feeding Sprocket, and Susie was working on homework. Writer scampered to the barn to spend some time with my wife. "Dad," Susie yelled, "is that you?"

"No, it's the boogie man."

"Very Funny. Can you come up here for a minute?" Susie's room was on the second floor.

"Lemme' grab a soda and I'll be right there."

I browsed through the mail: a dog fair reminder from our veterinarian, a Humane Society request for donations, and a request for my attendance at the new dog park groundbreaking. Do you get the impression that I'm a patsy for such appeals? *Timely*, I thought, considering what I had been involved with over the past few days. "Napoleon lives," I said to no one in particular.

I grabbed a soda from the fridge and headed up to Susie's room. "What's going on, Sugar?"

She sat at her computer in her nightgown, working on a school project. Susie follows after me. She loves animals, dogs, absolutely, but she loves *all* animals. Mumbles, her four-year-old cockatiel, sat on her shoulder. Webs, her hairy tarantula, salivated as it looked at me through its glass enclosure. Santa, the fattest cat this side of Alice in Wonderland, bundled itself on her bedspread. I nearly tripped over Turnover the turtle, and her three-dimensional ant farm could teach us all a lesson about organization and community effort.

"What's crackin'," I said.

"Dad," she said with a sigh, indicating that my attempt at teenage slang had flopped.

"Okay," I replied. "What-is-it-I-can-help-you-with-my-daughter?"

She sighed heavier. Then she said, "I've been thinking about Bubbles."

I got this feeling that the stars were all aligned...against me. "What's on your mind, Pumpkin?"

"You've always talked about doggie heaven. And I've always taken it for granted that doggie heaven was where dogs go to spend time with God."

"Yes, Susie...that's what I've always said."

"Is that what you believe?"

"Yes, more than ever, yes. Because of the wonderful friendship that Bubbles shared with us, I believe he deserves to be in doggie heaven. And I believe it is a place visited often by God."

"Do you believe God has a dog?"

What a great question, I thought. Leave it to a kid to come up with something about dogs that I had never considered. "If He loves dogs as much as you and I, then I suspect He's had one since the beginning of time."

"That'd be a pretty old dog, dad," she said and we both laughed.

Susie is just a young child, but like her mother, she has a way of setting you up for a zinger, and I knew one was coming my way.

"But what if God had a regular dog, like Bubbles?"

"I suppose He could have just about anything He wanted."

"If He had a regular dog like Bubbles, then after about ten or fifteen years, his dog would die...just like Bubbles."

She was painting me into a corner.

"In that case," I countered, "He's probably had lots of dogs over the centuries."

"And where do you think God's dogs go when they die...that is, considering they're already in Heaven?"

Checkmate.

"Doggie heaven," is all I could think to say. "Now, lights out, big day tomorrow." We hugged, I kissed her forehead, led her to bed, tucked her in, and quickly dimmed the table lamp, and scooted from the room before she could hit me with another left hook.

Just as I reached the top of the stairs I heard her yell out, "Thanks, dad."

"You're welcome," I yelled at her, thankful that the conversation was, at least temporarily, over.

I walked to the barn where Susan was finishing the last of her chores. Our barn and our horse are one and the same. Both are old and weathered; one moves slow and the other is slowly moving. Our barn, built 150 years ago, slumps more and more following every winter, its hand-hewn timbers are slowly giving way to the pressures of the snow, rain, and wind. Sprocket is slow to move, physically, and is sluggishly approaching her final day. She was my therapy horse after Jennifer died. I talked to her every day about my time with that wonderful lady. She always listened attentively, and I'd brush her aging coat while she ate.

When Susan and I got married, Sprocket was drawn to her as if she were the reincarnation of Jennifer. Imagine my luck; I have been married to two of the most compassionate women of all time.

As Susan turned off the lights, Writer tugged on her gloved hand, wanting to play. We kissed and while holding hands, we walked to the pond and sat in the swing. Writer had had enough water for the day and lay at our feet. Darkness was descending over the valley. I told her about my day, ending by saying, "Let me ask you a question."

She looked at me, her eyes soft and her mouth forming the slightest of smiles.

I told her about my talk with Susie. "So what's the question?" she asked.

"You know that I believe dogs are a special gift from God and that they were specifically chosen over every other animal to befriend us and to help us through difficult times."

"Yes," she said, "and I know that comes from your heart.

"In fact," I continued, "what if it was God's intention from the beginning of time to send dogs as little guardian angels, knowing how poorly we handle life's struggles?

"Sooo..." she said.

"Maybe dogs did not vie to be positioned at our side at all, maybe dogs knew from the very beginning that they were created for one purpose and one purpose only—that being to live and die at man's side."

Susan looked at me but did not respond.

"And if that's true," I continued, "then there has to be a special place for them...there has to be. God would not, could not, forsake the very animal that He specifically put here in order to help get us through the difficult life that He created for us."

"Settle down, Bill," Susan said. "You're getting all worked up over conjecture and supposition."

"And if that's true," I continued, "then Susie's got a point. God's dogs, patterned perfectly after ours, must have a special place of rest after death. In fact, maybe He didn't even have a dog for Himself until he realized what they were doing for us...and then He had to have one for...who knows... to guard the gates of Heaven. And before long, He'd want one at his side for all eternity. Hell, I don't know, Susan, am I going crazy?"

And then Susan did what wonderful people do for each other, and it's why I'm the luckiest man in the world. She put her arm around me, and, with all the sincerity in the world said, "In that case, Bill, there's more than one up there, 'cause every saint and angel would want one too."

THE LAST DAY

DAY 6

I awoke at 6:00 on the sixth day—remembering this to be the day that God created all the animals of the earth. My sixth day with Napoleon. God's sixth day of creation. What a remarkable twist of fate. Or am I being presumptuous in calling it that?

If I have been able to defend against all believers of the big bang theory as opposed to the uncaused cause, then surely I can accept the possibility that providence, or destiny, had a hand in these six days of my life.

Then again, consider:

There are between 100 and 400 billion stars in the Milky Way galaxy.

The Milky Way is only one of billions of galaxies in the universe.

The average distance between stars in the Milky Way is over four light years.

The age of the earth is estimated at 4.5 billion years.

Two hundred million years ago, mammals began roaming our earth.

Sixty-five million years ago, dinosaurs died out.

When did Homo sapiens first appear? According to science, the numbers of years vary—but its huge.

After reading these statistics, do you think what I am about to experience on this very day, at this very moment in time, is based on the luck of the draw, or would you agree that some higher power is involved?

I'm going with the higher power theory.

Quietly, hoping not to waken Susan, I dressed, splashed cold water on my face, brushed my hair and my teeth, and tiptoed to the bedroom door.

"Billy?" Susan whispered in her pet name for me.

"Yeah," I whispered back.

"Would you tell Napoleon hello for me?"

God, I love this woman! I tiptoed to the bed and kissed her. "What I'm really gonna tell him is that you think all the Saints in Heaven have dogs."

She fell back on the bed and pulled the covers over her face. She mumbled something, it was either "I love you" or "Fix your own dinner tonight!"

"Thanks for helping me last night...and for believing in me." I closed the bedroom door before she could reply.

Writer waited at the foot of the stairs in full anticipation mode. I feasted on toast, jelly, and milk, and then slung my pack over my shoulder. I failed to catch the screen door as it slammed shut, prompting me to wonder if I would be the same person when I would walk through it later today.

Most of us follow the same maze everyday of our lives. Left, right, straight, click the lever, get food, move to the next maze, right, left, straight, click the lever, and on and on and on.

But there are a few of us, just a few mind you, that demand new and challenging mazes every day of our lives. And we pay the consequences with bloody noses, banged up heads and hearts, broken bones, dashed hopes, and dreams shattered worse than Humpty Dumpty. Every now and then though, through the favor of God, we discover, or arrive, or get answers, or enter, or succeed, or we are granted, all because we see the world differently than most.

I briefly wondered how today's maze was going to affect me physically, mentally, and emotionally. But then again, not having the answers was a big part of the challenge. Everyone has the questions; no big deal. I had chosen to seek answers and I had no idea what was in store for me.

The morning was dark as we started up the hill, and then dead time took over my body, until I found myself at the door of the bog, having no memory whatsoever of the past fifteen minutes of my life.

I paused, not thinking about the past or future, only of the present moment in time; only of the present moment in my life. It is said that each of us has a moment in which our life's purpose will be revealed, and it is our response to that moment that is closely monitored. I wondered if the one monitoring all things was also noting my pause, my hesitation. If so, I wondered how that would be interpreted—an interpretation, however that would not affect my next breathe of life. And, as that thought passed, Writer and I stepped into the bush.

THE LAST MEETING

DAY 6

The bog had changed, or should I say *was* changing.

The brilliant colors were less brilliant. The bright reds and yellows were turning dull. Birds still sang, their songs mellower now, less energetic. The air was heavier and more difficult to breath. Trees once thick with leaves were slowly thinning. Only the blue spruce and green pines retained their colors.

Overall, the woods were turning pale. Even Writer noticed the change. She sniffed along the ground where she and her friends had sunned, raised her head into the layers of scent that lay above the ground, and then sat and howled an invitation. The trees and grass and water absorbed her call, and I wondered if any of it reached beyond our enclosure.

I sat on the tree stump and reviewed my list of questions, crossing out two and adding one. The one I had added would be the final question I would ask

Napoleon, and the importance of it had not come to me until this very minute.

Susan and I had spent at least three hours the night before, selecting topics as discriminatingly as humanly possible. I did not want to waste the slightest moment of time with Napoleon today—time that could never be replaced—time that might never present itself again.

Bonj came from the bush less frisky than other days, as if signaling the change that was becoming. Writer cautiously trotted to greet her friend, and opposed to prior days of romping and rolling on the ground, they touched noses and licked each other's face before their ritual of sniffing various parts of each other's body. A single butterfly absentmindedly crossed their path, and the two dogs took to the chase as if the "hound of the Baskervilles" had invaded their personal space.

"I wonder about our future when I see the antics of the pups of today," Napoleon said with concern, as she approached me from behind.

I laughed. "You don't know how many times I've heard that in the outside world—about kids, that is." But then I realized that had been the reference she was making."

She then turned her attention to more serious topics. *"There is an interesting story you should read sometime, it is entitled Eight Hours to Live."*

I wondered if she had been listening in on my recent thoughts about the concept of time. "I am familiar with it," I said.

"It tells of the Eight Principles of Time."

"Yes, I know."

"Which principle is your favorite?" she asked.

"Number one," I said, but I did not elaborate. I wondered if she knew all eight. She did!

"*That's the one about mortality; it states that time is measurable,*" Napoleon said.

"I already feel the tethering vines of mortality reaching for me," I said, "and truthfully it's the recipe for terrible nightmares."

"*We don't see it that way,*" she said. "*The principle merely asks that you use the time allotted between now and your death to the best of your ability.*"

She sat beside me. I'd swear leaves on trees within the bog were turning brown before my eyes and falling to the ground, laying a new mantel of soft crackling foliage that no intruder could quietly penetrate. I no longer wondered how she knew about books, and principles, and history, and the cosmos. I merely accepted it as fact. "What's your favorite principle?" I asked.

"*Both two and eight.*"

This time it was she who did not elaborate, forcing my memory to kick into gear. "Principle number two states that time is precious and priceless. It is only here for the moment, and then it is gone—forever!"

"*Very good,*" she said. "*Do you believe humans think about the concept of forever?*"

"No," I said. "It is too frightening. It is the food that feeds our second greatest fear, with the first being death itself.

"*And what is principle number eight?*"

How could I forget number eight? How could anyone who had read *Eight Hours to Live* forget number eight? It is a statement that shakes you to the core. It is the ice-cold slap of reality. It's the earth-shaking principle that wiped out the dinosaurs. "Time can be lost—forever," that word again...*forever!*

"I think time and change go hand in hand," she said. "Look at the change since the time of Christ, since the time of The Great War, since the time of Martin Luther King."

"I wish we could put time on hold. I wish we could stop the change," I said, without knowing why I had said it. And then I remembered a question, "How do dogs deal with time?"

"*Time is a human concept; it is not an animal concept,*" she said. "*To a great degree, animals merely exist.*"

"I don't understand."

"*Exactly, you can't. Time passes, but we pay it no mind because it is not part and parcel of who we are. It has no meaning to us. That is one of our gifts from the Maker. Imagine, if we had to deal with time—what that would do to us. Days staked in the yard, or left in a pen, or abandoned, or forgotten, or waiting to be adopted, or left out in frigid or scorching weather would be endless for us. We would literally die of heartbreak, loneliness, and fear. Therefore, we are not saddled with the idea of time. The same is said for such concepts as rationalization or intent or planning or expectation. Our responses to human interaction are based on genetics, conditioning, socialization, training, and affection.*"

I looked at her blankly. "A lot of my friends will not want to hear this. In fact, if I spoke your words the animal behaviorists and activists would hang me in effigy." And then I added, "Hopefully, only in effigy."

"*Then look at it this way. How about canine concepts that are beyond anything humans can conceive?*"

"Like what?"

"*Our senses are barely calculable by humans. Yes, you may deduce that our sense of scent is many times that of yours...but since you cannot actually experience the nth degree of the scent of a Bloodhound, then you may never truly know it. And let me tell you, you don't want to go there; it would drive the human nose to implode.*"

She paused and I waited; sensing she had more to say.

"*Many of you love us, a few tolerate us, and others have little care for us. We do not wish to be abused, we do not wish to be ignored, and we do not wish to be euthanized. Ours is a mission of brotherhood, a mission of passion, and a mission that defines our way of life.*"

"What do you think about?"

"*Again you attempt comparisons. If you are a tree, we are not the sapling. If you are a mountain, we are not the molehill. If you are the tiger, we are not the cub.*

"*Rather, think this way: if you are a tree, we are the rock. If you are a mountain, we are the sea. If you are the tiger, we are the dog.*

"*Our thoughts are comprised of what you see in us...not of what you THINK you see in us. We think of water and food, freedom, and of finding a mate. We think of protecting our well-being and of protecting our human master.*

"*There is little else for us to consider beyond those concepts.*"

"How do you communicate with one another?"

"*Certainly not as you and I are now exchanging thoughts and words. What you and I are sharing has* never happened, and may never again happen. Much of our communication is through touch. By watching us closely, you will see what I mean. We share food, protection, and caves. We heal our pack mates, we are dedicated to teaching our young, and we hunt as one. Is this not a wonderful form of communication?

"I do not understand why you are so willing to give up your life for us?"

I'd swear, for the first time in the short time I had known her, her lips tightened.

"The answer to this question is contrary to much of what I have told you and may be difficult for you to grasp."

"Try me," I said.

"At birth, we, each of us, are given the gift of momentary understanding. For the briefest flash in time, we are given a choice. In addition to the traits of our breed, we are offered an added ability, not necessarily an opportunity for the use of that ability, but rather an opportunity to possess the ability. It is an offering only and need not be accepted."

I did not understand and I told her so.

If she could scratch her head, I think she may have opted to do so. "Our choices are protection, alarm, search and rescue, companionship, to assist the disabled, and the offering of life. These are the ability choices, but remember; we do not know if the opportunity of exhibiting these abilities will emerge. It is purely a concept of wait and see."

I was apprehensive about asking for an example. She must have seen or heard my thought.

"The dog choosing protection may be called upon to stand between evil and his master. The dog choosing *alarm may be called upon to wake his human pack when fire strikes—"*

I could not refrain from interrupting. "And the dog choosing the offering of life?"

She answered my question with avoidance. *"Bear in mind, the opportunity may never present itself."*

I was shaken and a little miffed by what I was hearing. At birth, each dog receives an intimate connection with its maker, chooses, or not, a special ability which may or may not be needed in later life.

"It is the choice, you should know, that determines honor among all. Remember, the opportunity may never present itself, but a dog lives with the binds of that choice for all of his time."

"And for each choice, I suspect the dog receives a higher position in the afterlife...especially the poor guy who chooses to give up his life!" My question was meant to be cynical.

"That is correct."

"I was being sarcastic."

"Yes, I know."

Now I was more than a little miffed. "There are levels of afterlife?"

"Does that not seem reasonable to you? Consider the protection dog dying on the battlefield with his master, the alarm dog perishing in the fire, the security dog loosing his life while attacking a hostage taker. Do they not stand above the others?"

And then I understood the moment of revelation and decision that each pup was given at birth. "They also get to know the rewards of choice?"

"Yes, they do. Is this not something you have wondered about regarding humanity?"

I don't know how she knew. But she knew.

"Do you not believe that those dealing with pain, suffering, poverty, hunger, disabilities, and loneliness deserve a higher place in Heaven than those who abuse their gifts?"

"I do believe that," I said.

"And so it is with dogs."

I needed to stretch my legs. I walked to the pond, knelt, parted the top layer of dust that floated upon its' surface, and then put my head under. When I returned from the world of swimming things, both Bonj and Writer stood at the ready, hoping for a game of fetch. I looked out over the pond, its stillness barely disturbed by the ripples of my dunking. Mother Nature painted the reflection of the opposite wall of the bog upon the pond's face. I grabbed a ruler-size stick and heaved it with all my might. Moments later, Bonj and Writer left the dock as one, airborne, and then belly flopped within striking distance of their wooden prey.

Snap. My mind took a picture of their antics. This and many other moments of the past days would stay within my minds eye until the end of my time.

GOOD-BYES

DAY 6

I walked back to Napoleon. She had moved to the shade of a hundred-year-old maple tree. And then, as unbelievable as it sounds, the procession started. From behind every tree, rock, and thicket, animals appeared— the momma bear and her cub, deer, fox, rabbits, squirrels, possum, raccoon; and bringing up the rear of the cortege was Bonj and Writer. They did not wander about in a meaningless way; rather, they moved with intention...and the intention was to acknowledge Napoleon.

Each passed the Maple tree where she rested, momentarily paused, and then moved back to the fringes of the pond, where even the largemouth bass were shooting from the water and flopping back with what seemed like synchronized splashes. Birds of every feather swooped and sang their song, each trying to outdo the one before. Napoleon was known and revered by all animals! What I was watching was so far beyond human understanding that I became weak-kneed and had to sit at the edge of the shade.

When all had paid their respects, Napoleon said, *"There is one yet to come."* Her tone was such that I knew we would have to wait. But it was not for long.

A shuffling sound came from the direction through which I had entered the bog. Someone or something was having difficulty finding its way. Writer and Bonj bolted to the rescue and plunged into the wall of the bush.

I looked at Napoleon, expecting an explanation, but she ignored me, maintaining her steadfast composure.

Then, out of the bush came Writer and Bonj. My twenty-six-year-old horse, Sprocket, walked gingerly behind them. Arthritis is the only thing keeping her joints together. She is sway-back, almost toothless, and her hoofs are cracked and broken. She has such a difficult time getting around that we usually let her into the pasture only if Susan or I are with her.

It would be impossible for her to climb and descend the hill between the barn and the bog! And yet, miraculously, she was making her way towards Napoleon.

I looked at Napoleon and murmured, "Noooo."

But she would not look back. I ran to Sprocket, crying, imagining what she had endured to come here. Her breathing was labored, her legs bled openly from the puncture of the briars, and her neck could barely support her drooping head.

She allowed my hugs and then continued her walk of labor in the direction of Napoleon.

Low moans, howls, screeches, and wails were emitted from the animals and birds that now surrounded Sprocket. She could not make it to Napoleon before her legs gave out and she collapsed. She lay sprawled on the ground, gasping for air that could no longer sustain her lungs and her life. But she was where she wanted to be, with her friends, with Napoleon, with Writer, and with me. I lay on the ground beside her, carefully resting her head on my jacket, while embracing her as best I could. I whispered wonderful memories and heartfelt thanks into her ear while wiping my tears that dripped upon her face.

    Napoleon snuggled against Sprocket's chest and rested her head across the neck of the dying horse. I continued talking to her until her last breath, shallow and quiet, disappeared into the calls of the wild that would protect and guide her into the afterlife.

John Preston Smith

LEAVING THE BOG

DAY 6

Hours later, as I stood and watched, Sprocket was totally covered by plant life, twigs, brushwood and undergrowth that was brought and deposited by hundreds of birds. And their singing never stopped.

The celebration of her death and burial was as pure as any event I had ever witnessed and I wondered how I would do justice to the story I would share with Susan and Susie Q. How could I expect them to believe that Sprocket had made the trip to the bog when I could hardly accept it myself?

Writer nudged my hand and I scratched that favorite place behind her ear. There was no other animal life in the bog, save for Napoleon and Bonj, both of whom sat in the shade, watching. Where vibrant colors and sounds had once permeated the bog, now brownness had taken over. It was changing from what it was to what it would be, and I wondered if I would ever come back.

I returned to where Napoleon sat. "Thank you," I said, "she was a wonderful horse. She taught me much about humility by throwing me from the saddle anytime she didn't like where I wanted to ride."

"She was fortunate to live with people who appreciated another of the Maker's special gifts."

"We all should die as beautifully."

"Are there any final questions?" Napoleon asked.

Still shaken by what I had experienced, I had to resort to my list of questions. Three stood out above those remaining. Thinking about the past few days, I asked, "Why is it so difficult for humans to recognize miracles?"

There was no hesitation in her response. *"If I were asking the questions, that is one I would be asking you."*

Her answer did not surprise me, but it did disappoint me. I was hoping against hope that she would reveal the answer, maybe even the solution, to one of my personal struggles. I was supposed to be asking questions about her, and because I am human, I had strayed. It was an unjust question and I apologized to her.

"What do you represent?" I asked.

"Loyalty. We are our masters' keeper. When you are given to us it is a pact for life...for our life. There is no one in your life that you think about at all times. It is impossible for you. It is fully possible for us.

"As it has been planned, yours is a life of multiple purposes. You are to be both good and gentle. You are to love one another. And you are to aspire to the kingdom of God.

"Your brief time on earth, however, is challenging and demanding. It is full of days of wonder and nights of dread. For some of you, life is unbelievably short; for others, it endures for many years. You may be prosperous or you may be a pauper. Your fellow man may measure you as a success or judge you as a failure.

You may have been granted the elixir of health or the poison of sickness, pain, and suffering. Yours is a life of the oxen: you are burdened with the gift of choice, you must carry the yoke of life-defining decisions, and you must control the beast of desire.

"Loyalty, however, is the defining trait of our kind. We are a pack of the pact. We have accepted the one thought, the single purpose, and the just cause. Because of this, we think of you at all times.

"It is not our death that we fear, it is yours. We can deal with ours, we cannot live with yours. You have been granted multiple coping methods if your friend or family member passes. We have none. That is why we lay at the casket, at the grave, or beside your lifeless body. That is why our Master has granted us such a short life...because we cannot live if our best friend is lost...that is why our world is over so quickly.

"Our emotional tie with you is the same as was yours with Sprocket as she died.

"God made us so that we will always have to look up to you...He knows now that that is also our choice."

It was time for my last question...the question that had been haunting me most...and I didn't even know how to phrase it. "Why has this day come to be?"

"It is not important for you to tell the story of what you have experienced. Who, other than Susan, would believe you anyway? It is important, however, that you KNOW the story...because the day may come when you will be called upon to be our voice...and it may be your voice that determines our future as man's best friend. If you accept this burden for a challenge that may or may not present itself, it will surely affect your level in Heaven."

I did not hesitate to nod my head.

There was nothing else for me to say. I patted Bonj and thanked him for crying out to me on that first day. He did not act as if he understood what I said. He licked my hand, and along with Writer, took one final lap around the pond, a small body of water that now was covered in a greenish scum while a thicket of cattails had appeared along its shoreline.

I knelt down and hugged Napoleon while she licked my face.

I smiled when she said, "*I like the name.*"

She brushed against my leg before loping towards the pond. She nuzzled Writer, as did Bonj, and without looking back, headed for the bush at the far end of the bog. Just before they disappeared, I could see Bonj attacking the tail of her mom. They did not see me wave.

Writer, still at the pond, watched them leave. She looked back at me as if to ask what was happening. She looked back to where they had been and barked—a very high-pitched sound that was unsteady and unsure. The return was weak, but Bonj did answer. With that, Writer ran to me and sat by my side.

The bog had totally changed. Now, it was no different than any other thicket surrounded by all the growths and sounds of Mother Nature. I saw the unsteady flight of a last butterfly as she disappeared into the trees. A mosquito stung my neck.

I shouldered my backpack and headed for the door that would lead me from a place I would never visit again. A distant thunder warned of a stormy night, and long shadows pointed at me as if reminding me of a future responsibility.

Writer ran ahead and I paused at the point in the bush that had been my passageway to a world that I had never known existed.

It seemed appropriate to repeat the two words that had been my password into that world six days earlier.

"Thank you," I said. I listened. But there was no response. I said it again, louder. And a third time as loud as my throat would bear.

And then, as I took that first step into the bush, the faint sound of a howling wolf, somewhere deep in the woods, came to me.

It was a sound that I will carry with me until I see her again in the afterhere.

The End

John Preston Smith

LETTER TO MY READERS

MY DEAR FRIENDS:

It would be unfair for me to leave you without presenting the narratives *The Prophecy of Canine* and *The Stray* as mentioned by Napoleon in *The Bog*. I also want you to know that *Eight Hours to Live,* was taken from my book, *Beyond Imagination.*

You may surmise by my writings that I am not of the school of chance. Rather, I am of the school of order and design. I see purpose, and reason, and goodness in a world of continual sunsets, and rainbows, and newborn children whose sight, and hearing, and words are as pure as The Maker who formed them.

I believe The Maker also formed the galaxies, the earth where we live, and the animals that surround us. It is those animals, particularly dogs, which I see as our guardians, protectors, and companions. That being said, there has to be a beginning to all things. *The Prophecy of Canine* is what I see as the beginning of the relationship between man and his dog.

The Stray begs a particular question that has bothered me for many, many years. Why is it that so many dogs roam the streets hungry, cold, and unwanted? If reading my story encourages one individual to reach out to one of these creatures of God, then my belief in the goodness of mankind will be rewarded, and the One of Power and Grace will surely look upon that person with kindness and joy.

Thank you for reading my stories. JPS

The Prophecy of Canine

I cannot verify that the following is true. On the surface, it seems highly improbable, it questions man's individuality as the only soul-owner, and it may border on lunacy. If, on the other hand, you have personally encountered the blessings of this creature, if you have been touched by God's most compassionate hand, and this creation of His has entered your life, then for you, the improbable has become a reality. Read on, my friend, this story is for you.

♥♥♥♥♥

Although it is impossible to identify the exact year, 1000 BC seems likely. At that time, the animal kingdom realized that Man was God's creature of choice and that the only way of becoming a part of the eternal plan was through an alliance with this two-footed being. And so the Commune of All summoned a representative of every species. All would be given the opportunity to present their case, as to why they should be chosen to approach the Almighty, asking to be the one to stand equal to Man.

"I am king of the jungle," said Lion. "It is I that should approach the Powerful One. I will demand to be Man's earthly companion."

"And how would you present our case?" asked Wolf.

Said Lion, "I will show my power with a roar never before heard in all the land."

"But that sound was given you by the Powerful One. It surely will not bother Him, but it might strike fear into the heart of the one we want to befriend."

Rhino, that thick-skinned beast of the wild spoke next. "Who could withstand the menace of my charge? I will challenge the Powerful One with my might."

"Challenge, you say." Wolf shook his head. "That is not the approach we seek."

"He will shrink at the sight of my commanding tusks, the stomp of my massive feet, and the wail of my voice," said elephant.

"Not so," said wolf.

For the next seven hours, animals of each species demanded to be heard.

But nothing could be settled. Then, the beasts of size, strength, and supremacy—Lion, Elephant, Rhino, and Baboon—suggested that they be the Committee of Power that would approach The Almighty. "Surely, He will see that we are equal to Man," said Baboon.

"Absolutely not," said wolf.

Finally, one alone remained.

"How speak you?" asked wolf.

Canine walked forward, his head lowered by the weight of his thoughts, his body arched in confusion and frustration, his tail submissively dragging the ground. He stood before the assembly, slowly gathering his thoughts before he spoke. "Has not The Powerful One chosen Man as the ruler of the earth world?" he asked.

"That is true," responded wolf.

"Then, we are not looking to replace Man."

"That too is true."

"And since man alone was chosen by The Powerful One, I do not believe we should seek to stand as his equal."

All of the animals quieted, wondering at what Canine was saying.

"Rather, should we not be seeking a place at *the side* of Man," Canine offered, meekly.

The Commune of All quieted, and as each could, reasoned that Canine spoke what they all felt but had not been able to voice.

"What is it that you would do?" asked wolf.

"What is it that you would have me do?" asked Canine.

And then, throughout the night, Canine listened to his friends in order to prepare for his approach to the Holder of All Power.

More humbly than when he had first spoke, the Lion said to Canine, "I offer to share with you the goodness of my strength."

The Lamb offered meekness.

The giraffe offered surveillance.

The deer offered submissiveness.

The sparrow offered kindness.

The hawk offered his keenness of sight.

The cat offered indecision...it was the best he could tender.

Many others spoke, offering to share their speed, size, compassion, awareness, protectiveness, and companionship.

Canine listened to his friends, humbly accepting what each had to offer.

When morning came, every animal was exhausted, and so they slept—except Canine. He wandered the forest, lost in reflection, wondering at his difficulty. "What is the matter with me?" he asked the trees, and grass, and wind. "Who am I to approach the Lord God? Why would He listen to me? Why would Man listen to me? What is it that I really have to offer that Man needs? I cannot offer wealth, material goods, or success? I can only offer friendship, and loyalty, and dedication...things that Man can get from other Men."

"Maybe Man is in need of you as much as you are of him?" said Tree.

"But why would Man have need of animals?" replied Canine.

"Did you not just mention friendship, and loyalty, and dedication?" said Flower.

"But his friends?" questioned Canine.

"Man's friends are not always friends. They are not always loyal. Their allegiance, at times, is weak," said Wind. "You are the true representative of all species of animals, the true definition of friend. How could the maker of trees, and flowers, and wind not listen to you? And since He made of you what you are, since He is the Knower of All Things, maybe at this very moment, He is anxiously awaiting your knock at the door of the Great Mansion."

As Wind had been speaking, Canine's stature grew. The double coat of hair covering his body glistened as if freshly oiled. His ears stood erect, his chest expanded, his tail straightened, its tip barely touching the grass of Mother Earth. His proud figure offered strength, confidence, and humility.

He returned to the Commune of All as all had awaited his return.

"If the Maker of all Things will grant me an audience, I will represent each of you as best I can," he said. "Further," he continued as he surveyed the kingdom of animals, "are we in agreement to support, without question, the decision of our King?"

There were no dissenters.

"Thank you," said Canine. Then, with nothing left to say, he left the forest, his friends, and his home, setting out on a journey that would forever affect the future of both canine and human alike.

♥♥♥♥♥

Canine had not heard of The Council of Decision. He did not know of anyone who had ever appeared before its Tribunal.

He patiently waited in the vestibule of The Great Hall for what seemed an eternity when the enormous doors swung open and he was summoned to enter.

The magnificent auditorium was packed as far as the eye could see, as were the balconies, which extended to heights beyond sight.

And there he stood, alone. A few Clouds of Comfort had been permitted to float above the proceedings.

"Why have you asked to see the Father?" the voice said.

He pleaded the case of those who had appointed him. His final expression sought consideration for all. "Every species wants to be a friend to the Man. Each is as deserving as is the next," he said.

"If all are deserving, then why is it that you stand here alone?" asked the voice.

"I have been asked by the Commune of All to present our request to the Father."

"That you have done, my canine friend, for it is I to whom you are speaking," said the Lord.

Canine then curled on the floor, fearful of the wondrous sight before him. Every being present took in the beauty of the moment, basking in the light and love of His resplendent presence. It was Heaven's most fulfilling experience.

The Voice came forth. It was soft and soothing. "Canine, as you have done this for the least of your brethren, so too is it done unto me." He then called to Canine, "Come and sit at my side, best friend."

Canine sprang to his master and sat at his feet.

"It is no small thing that you ask," said the Father. "Man can be pure of heart. But he also can be fickle and forgetful. He does not always spare the rod. He can be vain, vulnerable, and manipulative. If you are to be his friend then you must accept him as he is; you must accept both his strengths and his weaknesses. Is that what you wish?"

Canine just leaned against the leg of his Lord.

"We will see," said the Father.

Canine was then tested. He had to survive without food and water. He had to endure cold and rain, heat and thirst, and months without so much as a single word of kindness. He was caged, chained, and physically abused.

Finally, in an ultimate test, Canine had to prove his friendship and dedication to Man by giving his life to protect the one he wished to serve.

♥♥♥♥♥

Therefore, it was not Canine that returned to the forest of the Commune of All. Rather, it was an Angel of the Lord. "Canine has been chosen," the angel said. "He has proved himself beyond all doubt. It is he who is to help Man through the difficulties of life. He came to the Maker buoyed by each of your gifts."

The animals milled about. Looking at one another with pride.

"And because of that Community Offering, I bring you these words from your Maker. He thanks you and promises to watch over you, even unto the smallest of his feathered friends. And secondly, it is your love of one another that has touched your Maker. And so, your brother Canine returns to you."

Having spoken these words, the Angel faded, as did the aura of light that had enveloped him.

The quiet of the moment froze all. No one breathed, nor moved, nor blinked.

And then, what seemed far in the distance was a Call of the Wild. And as it grew stronger, carried by wind whipping through the trees, every animal joined in a cacophony of sound whose beauty surely carried to the ear of the Lord.

And when Canine burst from the forest floor and into the midst of his animal friends, there was, it is said, a celebration beyond imagination.

But then again, maybe it's just a story!

The End

The Stray

"When the man waked up he said,

What is Wild Dog doing here?"

And the Woman said,

"His name is not Wild Dog any more,

but the First Friend,

because he will be our friend

for always and always and always."

—Rudyard Kipling

Life had been tough for Sammy. Not that he expected better, more that he didn't know that there was better. He was one of seven at birth, born on a wintry night under a farmer's chicken coop. Two of his sisters, weak and sick, were thrown into the snow by his mother.

At six weeks of age, his mother died and the others were taken away. For two years, tethered by chain to a rotting Maple tree, his world extended thirty feet. His protection against the elements was his tightly curled body and determination to survive. His nourishment consisted of table scraps, his table was the bare ground, and his drinking water puddled in holes when it rained.

He did, however, have a friend. The boy from the house came to see him late in the afternoons. The boy would watch and laugh as he ran in circles, jumping and barking. Then the boy would untangle him from the tree and sit beside him while he set his head in the boy's lap. The boy would pet him and tell him that he was a good dog. It was the greatest part of the day. Life could not be better.

When the snow fell, the boy stopped coming. Sometimes, it would be days before anyone threw scraps to him. He began to lose weight, and it was difficult to stay warm in the dropping temperatures.

He saw the boy one more time. The boy did not run out to play with him; instead he walked slowly. The boy talked to him in a voice he had not heard before. The boy stuttered in a soft, whispery tone. He saw water on the boy's face when the boy bent over and patted him. The boy fed him cookies and made whimpering sounds before leaving. That night, there were no lights in the house.

The next day, the house was silent. No one brought him food. He had wrapped himself around the tree and could barely move. The cookies were gone, he could not reach the frozen water, and he was colder than he could remember.

He knew—knew he had been left alone. Left to fend for himself or to die.

That night the fire warmed him. It melted the snow that covered his lean body, and he lapped at the droplets of water. But the heat became intense, and he sensed fear. When he looked at the house, he saw flames flying into the air and disappearing into the night.

Trucks came and sprayed water onto the fire and the old house crumbled to the ground, spewing hot coals that burnt parts of his coat. He yipped and barked until one of the masked men in a heavy black coat came running at him with steel on a stick. He wanted to fight him, but his weakness pulled him down and he waited for the sound of death.

The rusting chain broke free from the tree with one swing of the fireman's axe. The man removed his glove, offered his hand for Sammy to smell, and then patted him on the head. "Come on boy, let's get you outta here." He dragged the chain and followed the man out of the fenced yard that had been the boundaries of his world. People grabbed at him and he knew they would tether him to another tree, in another fenced area. He fought to get away.

"I got him," one man yelled, but then yelled again when the hot chain burned his skin. Sammy ran. The scent of water drew him in the direction of the river. His chain rattled on the bricks and blood trickled down his chest as it dug into his neck. He was hungry and thirsty and weak. But he did not stop. His run slowed to a jog, and then to a labored walk, but his heart raced. He was almost there, he could feel it, could almost taste it...water.

He stumbled into the stream that fed into the river before he knew it was upon him. It was cold, freezing, and it rushed the sting of adrenaline throughout his body. He laid in it, letting the wintry water cool his burned skin and singed hair. He stood and shook as hard as his drained body would allow.

At the edge of the water was a gutshot groundhog. He ate until the pains of hunger left his stomach.

He walked a short distance along the creek bed until he found an outcropping of brush that formed a lean-to. Dragging his chain, he burrowed through the scraggy bush into a small area that was both dry and sheltered from the wind. He meant to rest only momentarily, still sensing a need to get further away from the tree that had staked him to the ground. But his stomach was full, his exhausted body demanded rest, and fatigue overcame his desire to run. He walked in circles, patting the weeds into a nest, dropped to the ground, and curled tightly, sharing the heat with all parts of his body.

♥♥♥♥♥

The morning after the fire, I felt like someone had beaten me with a stick. I awoke with a start, the sound of sirens still ringing in my ears, my vision still blurry from the smoke, my lower back reminding me to let the younger firemen unfurl the hoses next time.

But the old ways were gone, never to return. It used to be that after we had responded to a fire, I would come home and Betty would be waiting to take care of me. She would have drawn a warm bath, laced with Epsom salts, and I'd soak for an hour of more, washing away the dirt and grim of burning buildings, of legacies lost, of lives changed forever. Fire does that. Then over cups of cocoa, I'd pour out my feelings about what I had encountered. It was a ritual as necessary as breathing.

My dad and granddad had been firemen. Granddad died in the line of duty. Dad fell from a ladder and broke his back. Miraculously though, he was not paralyzed, but it was a career-ending injury.

I was a fireman when Betty and I were married, and I admitted my weakness the first day we fell in love. I still remember exactly what I had told her. "After we respond to a fire, I will need to talk," I had said.

"About what?"

"About what it does to me, inside. I love being a fireman, but the death and destruction is sometimes difficult for me to handle. It might be something you won't want to deal with."

I remember that Betty smiled and kissed me, kinda like she was proud of me. "We'll see," she said, "we'll see."

For twenty years, she was always there when I needed her. Always a warm bath, always cocoa, always waiting to listen. That ended two weeks ago, when the flames of cancer took her away. Last night was my first fire without her.

When I got home and closed the door, I almost called her name. There was no aroma of cocoa, no bath, no one to talk with.

The next morning, I fought the urge to stay in bed. In our town, first responders to a fire are given the next day off. It may sound strange, but you would understand if you were a fireman.

Personally, I have never used that time for rest and relaxation. Instead, I have always visited the scene of the day before. Don't ask me why. Maybe it's to reaffirm what I do, trying to save property and lives from destruction. Mostly, it makes me feel better, especially if lives have been saved.

Today, however, I had to return to the scene because I had left something behind, and I felt guilty about it.

Only smoldering embers remained of what had been a three-story frame house in the lower-income section of our town. Investigators sifted through the ruins, attempting to find the cause. I was told the house was both empty and vacant, meaning that no one lived there and all personal property had been removed.

Firemen attending the blaze had knocked down most of the wooden fencing surrounding the property. I approached the tree where the dog had been chained and removed my axe, hoping no one had noticed I had left it behind. I had taken a mighty swing knowing I had to cut through a thick chain that had imprisoned a dog that would surely be burned alive. I had embedded my axe deep, and the heat from the fire had not allowed me to remove it. Now the handle was black; having been singed by the heat. All reasoning aside, I felt like a cop who had lost his gun in a fight.

Axe in hand, I returned to my car, embarrassed, under the smiling faces of the inspectors. Some things in life go best unsaid.

Before driving away, I looked back at the remains of the house and of the Maple tree. The tree was the size of one of those playground merry-go-rounds with rounded steel bars that kids can run and push and jump on and off. About two inches of the base of the tree was gorged out from the chain that had tethered the dog. There was one rusted pail. If it were for food where was the water bowl?

"Were they coming back for him?" I whispered. "Did they leave him to die?" Lastly, I wondered what had happened to him. After chopping him loose, he ran at my side, alluding the flames and heat. I remember he barked at me when his chain snagged against the fallen fence, and I returned and freed him a second time. When we cleared the yard and I cleared my eyes, I could hear his chain banging against the cobblestone as he ran. And then he was gone.

I thought of Betty and how she couldn't drive into town without picking up a stray animal, or moving a turtle to the side of the road, or putting a baby chick back into its nest. She had left me. And so had the dog.

The Bog, The Legend of Man's Best Friend

♥♥♥♥♥

Sammy awoke in the early morning of his first day of freedom. He knew nothing about being free, but this was it, and he had to deal with it. It had, however, its limitations, its yoke. The night before, he had been dragging a 15-foot chain that dug into his neck every time it caught on something. He could feel the crusted blood, pinching, itching.

He felt a tug on the chain. He froze. Then something yanked the chain and he yipped as it dragged him. He fought, digging his feet into the soft ground, while the shackle tightened around his neck and broke the crust of blood. The pain screamed at him.

"Got something here," the man yelled.

"What is it?" someone yelled back.

"A long chain. Should bring a couple of bucks. Must be tied to something heavy 'cause it's barely moving."

"Hold on." The second man dropped his bag of aluminum cans and ran to help."

Sammy relented. The pain was too much. His brief experience of freedom would end; another tree would soon dictate his life. He tunneled from under the brush and faced the men.

"Well I'll be," said the man who held the chain.

"Has to be the dog from the fire," said the second. "He's bleeding and burned."

Both men knelt down and talked to Sammy. One offered him a piece of biscuit.

Sammy was unsure. Their voice had that nice sound. Like the boy who used to visit. And the chain no longer pulled at him. He was hungry, friendless, and trapped. He scrunched down and crawled to them.

"Atta boy."

He stretched for the biscuit like an untrusting wolf. He ate while watching the men, wondering what they would do next.

Billy reached out and gently patted the dog on the head, removed the bandana from around his neck, walked to the river and soaked it, and returned and sat beside the dog. He slipped the chain from Sammy's neck and gave it to Donnie. "Throw it in the bushes," he said. "We don't want to recycle something that's used for pain and torture, do we?"

"Can't believe someone would chain a nice dog like this," Donnie said.

"Happens all the time," Billy wiped at the blood crusts on Sammy's neck.

"Then why do they get a dog?"

Billy thought about the last two statements that Donnie had made. Maybe Donnie wasn't the sharpest knife in the drawer, but he sure understood important things. "They shouldn't, Donnie. They shouldn't"

Sammy relaxed as the man cleaned his sores. He couldn't believe the chain was gone, that they slipped it from his neck so easily. How did they do that? One man chains him to a tree and another frees him. He couldn't understand how he let that happen for such a long time when all he had to do was back out of the chain. He leaned forward and licked the man's hand.

"Okay, here's the deal, big boy. Donnie and I have a full day of work ahead of us if we want to eat tonight."

"Chunky chicken?" his friend asked.

"Chunky chicken it is," Billy said to his friend.

Donnie ran to retrieve his aluminum cans.

"You, however, have a decision to make," he said to the dog, talking to him as he would to anyone else. "Donnie and I live the free life. We scrum for cans and metal, sleep under the bridge, don't bother nobody...and don't pay no taxes. We wash in the river, drink rainwater, smoke a little, and on Sundays we treat ourselves to fresh doughnuts." He paused. The dog cocked his head as if listening, as if understanding. "You're welcome to tag along if you want. We'll make sure you have a decent meal, and a warm place to sleep, and no chain. But, it's up to you."

Billy picked up his plastic bag of cans, petted Sammy, and walked away on the snow-covered hardpan along the river. He did not look back. He just repeated himself, "It's up to you."

Sammy watched the two men as they rambled along the river, their friendly chatter dissolving in the wind—the same wind that brought a familiar scent to his nose. He took one last look at his friends, barked, and then turned in the direction of the scent.

♥♥♥♥♥

After retrieving my axe, I headed for the city pound. There was a chill in the wind as tiny snowflakes drifted across the windshield, heralding a heavier afternoon snow. I doubted the stray had been picked up and taken to the animal shelter, but I was drawn there anyway. Maybe it was because the best dog I ever had was a stray. Maybe it was because Betty would have wanted me to check the shelter. Maybe it was because I needed companionship.

Or maybe it wasn't about me at all. Maybe I was worried about him. Was his chain caught on something, imprisoning him again? Was he freezing? Was he badly burned or bleeding and in need of help? Was he thinking that all humans were like his former owners?

The pound was just outside the town limits, at the end of a gravel road, next to the city dump. It was hidden so the town's people would not have to deal with the scraggly dogs and cats that arrived daily, or the barking and wailing, or the death and disposal.

A chain-link fence surrounded the two-acre field cluttered with outdoor dog runs. Metal or vinyl roofing covered each. A small building housed both office space and reception area. There was no indoor area for dogs. Both the city and county say there was no money for such extravagance.

Not that they would want to, but no one sneaks up on the city dog shelter. At the first crackle of gravel under the tires of an arriving vehicle, all hell breaks loose. I know dogs are not reasoning or rationalizing beings, but it's like they know this is their chance for a new life, and every dog in the place is barking the same message, "pick me, pick me, please pick me."

Oscar had run the shelter for twenty years, had found homes for thousands of dogs, and only put dogs down when the facility was over crowded and the city fathers demanded it.

We shook hands. "Richard, I was really sorry to hear about Betty's death."

Over the years Betty had been a consistent contributor to the shelter.

I thanked him for his thoughts and then told him about my stray and described the dog as best I could.

"Let's have a look see," he said.

Immediately, I knew two things. One, my stray wasn't here. No matter how many dogs were at the shelter, Oscar always knew about every one of them. Two, he was trying to bait me. And although it was difficult, I turned down his offer of a free dog or cat.

"Gonna try to find the fire-dog, uh?" he mused.

I shrugged.

We shook hands again. "I'll call if he turns up, Richard."

I thanked him and drove back along the gravel road, listening, but the dogs had stopped barking, as if knowing another chance had been lost. A thought played with my mind. Why had I considered him *my* stray?

♥♥♥♥♥

The biscuit had revitalized Sammy's endurance and his sense of smell led him back into the town he desperately abandoned the night before. Unencumbered by the chain, he had a new perspective on life. The burns on his body and the gash in his neck needed to heal, but mostly, he moved without pain.

He darted from the street when a car screeched its tires to avoid hitting him. A large dog lunged at him, snarling and growling, and would have seriously injured him had its owner not restrained it. Kids on bikes threw rocks and chased him into an alley before laughing and riding away.

He rested in a dark doorway as a truck slid its arms around a metal box, raised it in the air, shook it wildly, and then placed it back on the ground. A half-eaten hamburger rolled up to him and he ate. He followed the truck from the alleyway, raised his nose to the air, found the scent, and continued on his journey.

The downpour of snow thickened and two hours later he was about to loose the scent that layered in the air, when it led him to the red building. He wasn't sure what to do, but his sense of smell stopped him. Behind the structure, he found a plastic bag, tore into it, and found pizza crusts, old toast, and stale doughnuts. Of course, he didn't know what he was eating. No matter; it was tasty and filling, and satisfied his craving. As he licked at the fallen snow, he heard the slide of the bolt on the steel door. He found an opening in the lattice surrounding the deck and watched the man as he descended the steps.

"Well, for mercy sake," he heard the man say as he scooped up the trash and deposited it into a can. "Darn stray dogs outta be shot."

Fortunately for Sammy, he did not understand what the man had said. He knew it wasn't the man who had freed and patted him. The scent was different. But the man he was looking for had been here. And although the scent was gone, it had been locked in his memory, and he would recognize it when the man returned—if he returned. He decided to wait. He moved further under the porch, found a stack of papers, pawed them into a nest, curled and napped.

♥♥♥♥♥

Many coincidences in life go unnoticed, like running out of milk and cereal at the same time, or forgetting keys but finding the door unlocked, or arriving late for work on the day the boss is out sick.

But what about the more obvious ones, like being at the wrong spot at the right time, or finding the love of your life when you're not even looking, or facing death and being saved by a stranger?

Is it fate, destiny, luck, fortune, doom, chance, or coincidence? Do some things happen without an equal and opposite reaction? If you find happiness because of a right turn in life, would you have faced misery by turning left?

Why are some folks born rich while others live in poverty, some diseased while others live years of happiness? Is a person fortunate or unfortunate to hit the lottery, to gamble successfully, or to speculate on the market?

How is it that some seem blest, gifted, or chosen, while others fight mental, emotional, or physical disabilities?

Why are some saved and others lost, some live while others die, some rescued while others burn alive?

For those who suffer, is there some unseen hand of mercy that finally steps in and declares enough is enough?

None of these thoughts played on Sammy's mind. The scent of the man who had saved him, the man who had offered his hand, and the man who had patted his head, had led him to where he now waited. And that's all there was to it.

♥♥♥♥♥

Sammy woke at the sound of the steel door opening. He was shivering. The wind gusted hard enough that the falling snow stung his frail body.

A man walked from the door with a large can, carrying it towards one of the oversized metal bins.

A wisp of familiar scent teased the dog ever so slightly. He stood, stretched, and raised his nose into the air. There it was again. He stepped forward, whiffed slowly, and the scent strengthened. Nature took over. The dog did not monitor his movement; the scent did. Moments later he found himself inside the building, surrounded by huge trucks, much like the ones he had seen the night before at the fire.

He heard the man returning up the steps, walk into the room, and slam and lock the metal door. He was too exhausted to run, but to where? Again, he was trapped.

And then he saw his out. The door of every truck was open. He picked the closest one, gathered his strength, and lunged.

The scent was as strong as the night before. It came from a coat on the back seat. He scratched at it until it fell. He stood on the coat, basking in the aroma of the man who had saved his life. He walked on the coat in a tightening circle, slowly lay down, and rested his head on his rear legs.

He was hungry; but he felt good. His skin still burned; but he felt safe. He was cold; but warmth was moments away. And so he slept.

♥♥♥♥♥

After grabbing a sandwich at Kelly's Diner, I headed for home, my mind in a stupor about the day's events. "*Keep looking,*" my wife spoke to me, nudging me more in death than when she lived at my side.

"He'll be fine," I said aloud as I passed the still-smoldering rubble of last night's fire. I circled the block and pulled to the side of the road. One of the investigators motioned to me as I entered the yard behind the house; he was holding a burnt piece of wood.

"You looking for Sammy," he said as we shook hands.

"What are you talking about, Jimmy," I said.

He handed me a piece of charred lumber into which the name Sammy had been roughly scratched; the letters irregular and uneven. It was still warm to the touch and I wondered if the child who had whittled it was missing Sammy as much as I.

"It was nailed to the old Sycamore that fell during the fire," Jimmy said. "Good thing you broke him loose or he'd be a goner." Jimmy walked back into the rubble, continuing his job of digging it out, trying to find the source of the fire.

"You looking for Sammy?" the same question Jimmy had asked, this time, came from behind me.

I turned to see two men standing on the sidewalk. "Pardon me?" I said back, not knowing which one had spoken.

"After you cut him loose, he high-tailed it thataway," the man with the pipe said as he pointed toward the river. "His singed hair was smokin' and he was still pullin' that chain they used to tether him to the tree." The man was shaking his head.

"Damn shame if you ask me," the second man said. "They kept him chained night and day and fed him little more than bread and water. Then they move away and leave him behind like he was a piece of the house they was rentin.' It ain't right, I tell you, it just ain't right."

"Think you'll find him?" The man with the pipe asked.

Before I could answer the other man said, "That pup sure deserves a good home."

With that they turned and walked away, leaving me with the feeling that more responsibility had just been loaded on my shoulders.

"Keep looking," my wife said again.

This time I didn't respond. Instead, I started walking toward the river.

Slowly, ever so slowly, as I neared the water, the freshness of the river wavered in the breeze and overtook the taste and smell of the burned house. It was a welcome reprieve. Snowflakes, bigger than silver dollars, landed and disappeared on the two inches already covering the ground. It was the most unusual winter I had encountered. How can you possibly describe the feel of snow and sand underfoot…at the same time?

I walked along the water, maybe fifty yards, before I saw it. It was so out of place I knew it had to be the same one. I picked it up, turned it over in my hands, and could see the crusted blood around the part that had encircled Sammy's neck. I brought it to my nose; the scent of burning hair and skin scalded the lining of my nostrils.

As best I could, I dug through the snow and sand, put the chain in the hole, and covered it over.

"I set him free."

The voice startled me and I jumped up.

"Found him this morning, removed the chain, and invited him to join us."

"So did I," I said.

"I don't understand," said the beach comber."

"I set him free from the tree where he had been chained," I explained.

"You buried the chain?" One of them said.

"Yeah."

"We didn't want it either. It'd bring a coupla bucks at the junk yard, but I don't think God wants us to profit offa something like that."

"Have you seen him since this morning?" I asked.

"Nah. That's the reason we backtracked. Hopin' to see if he was still around. We liked him. Dog been through that kind of hell and still lick your hand...well, that says something about his character...know what I mean?"

I did and I told them so.

"You lookin' for him too?"

I was and I told them so.

"Good for you, man," they said in unison. The looked at each other and laughed. "Hope you find him," the quieter man said. "He'll make a good pet."

With that, they waved, shouldered their bags of cans, and wandered along the riverbank kicking at the snow, reveling at the life before them.

I thought about Sammy and his decision not to join these two friendly men. He must have headed back towards town. But where would he go? The only place he knew was where he had been chained and no one there had seen him. *Where else would he go*, I wondered. Would he try to find the scent of the boy who had fed him? I had heard of stories where dogs would travel cross-country to find a friend. Could this be one of those stories in the making?

And then I heard it. That unmistakable sound that piques the adrenaline, that high-pitched shrill that pierces the night or day with alarm; the station was signaling firemen to action. It was my day off. But, in reality, firemen do not believe in such a thing when the alarm sounds. Instinctively, I reached for my cell phone, but had left it in the car. My jog broke into a run, which broke into a sprint. I made it to the car in less than two minutes. I speed-dialed the station and gave my location.

"The pumper just pulled out, should be passing you in sixty, they'll slow and you hop aboard," cap told me.

By the time I grabbed my axe and made it to the corner, I could hear the truck coming. I began to jog in the street so the truck would not have to stop; the air breaks hissed as the pumper slowed and I hopped aboard.

I jumped in the back seat and reached for my coat, and there, curled in a tight knot and sleeping through all the turmoil, was Sammy. "Is this a joke?" I yelled at the guys in the front.

Jasper Billings, my friend of twenty years, turned. "Well I'll be damned. How'd that mutt get in here?"

"You mean you guys didn't know?"

"Swear to God," he said while signaling the Boy Scout sign.

But all was not well. Sammy was shivering and barely breathing. Could he have been looking for me the whole time I was looking for him? That didn't make sense. Dogs can't do that! But, still...

I knew he was exhausted. He looked dehydrated. And as I talked to him he did not move. "My God," I said, "I think he's dying."

"False alarm, false alarm," the two-way belched. "Bring 'em back home."

I touched Sammy. He couldn't even raise his head.

Right when he had found the person who had saved him, right when he might have a new home, Sammy faded. His body had taken all that it could. He couldn't even muster the strength to respond as his newfound friend spoke to him.

But there was a new feeling taking over his body as his heart slowed. And in the new light, he could swear that he saw many of his kind running towards him from the Commune of All. He had always dreamed of this place, but never in his wildest dreams could he have known it was real.

And then he felt the man's touch, and a voice calling to him, and the light disappeared.

♥♥♥♥♥

"You won't believe this," Jasper yelled to Richard.

"What!"

"It's the County Veterinary Clinic...the false alarm is at the vet clinic."

Doc James was already outside, talking to the men in the first truck. He had inadvertently tripped, and while falling grabbed the alarm switch by mistake.

Jasper was already out of the truck and running to James, while Richard whisked Sammy into his arms and followed behind. James looked at Sammy and knew the dog was dying. "Follow me," he said and the three men ran into the clinic.

♥♥♥♥♥

Two days later, I was driving home from the vet with Sammy lying at my side, his head in my lap.

"Thanks, Betty," I said. "A false alarm at the vet clinic. Only you could do that!"

And from somewhere far in the distance, I heard her gentle voice speak to me. *"Take good care of Sammy,"* she said.

"I will," I said as Sammy licked my hand. "I promise."

The End

ALSO BY JOHN PRESTON SMITH

NONFICTION:

14000 Dogs Later, My Life With Dogs and What I've Learned

NOVELS:

Murder on the Trap

Never Again

Master of the Shadows

Beyond Imagination

CONTACTS:

Web site: www.jprestonsmith.com

FB: www.facebook.com/thebogthelegend

Twitter: @harlyman60

Blog: www.thebogblog.com

Instagram: HARLYMAN60

Made in the USA
Charleston, SC
28 February 2015